I'm Just Going Down
To The Pub
To Do A Few Miracles

Also By Colin Bloy and Suzanne Thomas

Who'd Have Thought It (2017)
(Amazon eBook)

Other articles and booklets by Colin Bloy
to be found on website
https://www.fountaininternationalmagazine.com
Free quarterly Magazine and monthly Newsletter

I'm Just Going Down
To The Pub
To Do A Few Miracles

Colin Bloy

Edited by Suzanne Thomas

Editor's Foreword

For many, this seems to be a long-awaited republication of a modern classic, and as I have gone through the book, I have felt that the information held within its pages is dynamite, and it is very timely to bring it back out into the public domain.

Colin Bloy was a special man for his research, and testing experiments, adding much information to his chosen subject. He would never claim to be a miracle worker and as a healer, would be extremely embarrassed if you called him that.

(In fact, all miracles and magic, are just things that we don't understand the workings of yet.)

In this book Colin writes in a matter of fact way about healing, and how it can be rational, in the way that it is done, and normal to do, using the knowledge and techniques held within here.

I qualified as a healer in 1981, and was taught it, as a transference of energy, and we were just channels for Pure Love energy, which flowed through us to the patient. To my way of thinking Colin took this on a stage further, with his experiments and dowsing, giving us a framework to work with healing.

For the beginner, who knows nothing about healing, a very basic, simple thing to do, with no technicalities, is to channel vital energy to boost the energy levels of a sick person. Details of which come in the chapter, "Giving Vital Energy."

Join Colin on his journey of discovery in the field of healing. See how he developed his healing skills, learn about the energy bodies and archetypes, this is a rare expedition. But you too can follow in his footsteps, if you have a pure desire to be of service to others, and practise.

This book should be required reading for all want to be healers and healers, who want to refine the ways in which they work. It is a pure treasure trove.

Enjoy
Suzanne Thomas
June 2019

To all those with a pure desire to heal.

Contents

Chapter 1

Know Yourself

Who are you? That may sound a facile question. But who are you? Amanda Jones or John Smith? As Colin Wilson once said in "The Outsider", most of us can look in our wallets and find some kind of identification – it's comforting. My driving licence says I'm Colin Bloy, but does it really help me? It's compartmentalisation, and does not help me to identify my essence or know it. The only thing it tells me is that I have a reference for bureaucratic purposes.

Who am I? Who are you? If you have asked these questions and have decided to become self-aware.

WELCOME TO THE CLUB.

You see it's alright. Actually, you are not alone. If you are waking up simply by reading this text, again I say, "Don't worry, you're not alone." Thousands have crossed the bridge. The first who did were terribly frightened and with reason. They were pioneers into the realms of consciousness, and it was lonely, peering into that particular void. Jesus, who was also a legitimate pretender to the throne of Israel, but that's alright, it doesn't make him somehow less sacred – was a highly evolved man, and when he was properly prepared, the Christ entered into him – the Cosmic Christ, (see Edouard Schure on the subject.)

He was wakened up, although he knew where he was going, and in a sense, I believe that sort of waking up was rather like Ouspensky's description of being at one with the elements in a storm. It's reflected in many of the romantic poets when you've made it. You are at one with the universe, with nature. It's not soppy sentimentalism, it's real identification.

Chapter 2

Self-Awareness

That's terrifying if you don't have it under control. Self-awareness, when it comes on, is often rejected, and may sometimes be interpreted as a psychologically negative condition. Some simply crawl back to their bureaucratic departments, labelled with their names. It's much easier. They know who they are!

Gurdjieff said "I have not come to teach. I have come to wake people up." Well, aren't we asleep most of the time?

Waking up is dangerous and exciting. It means we aren't any longer manipulated by the collective consciousness, the received wisdom, the way others think – we are suddenly ourselves. But that's tough, because we are alone. Really alone. Real loneliness. You are alone in the whole universe, you are not Colin Bloy CJAW 98:4, which is my wartime identity number. You're something else, you are aware of BEING. Not a number, not a name.

The psychiatric hospitals are full of people who become self-aware, clairvoyant, clairaudient, clairsentient, and they get dismissed with all sorts of categories. Schizophrenia, for one, is a convenient dustbin in which to dump people who wake up, don't understand, and are clairaudient. I speak from very specific experience.

It is my humble opinion that psychiatry is the worst of the pseudo sciences, not because of charlatanism, but because of using the wrong model to describe the true nature of consciousness, and I sympathise with contemporary psychiatrists.

Sadly, the usual remedy for so called psychiatric disturbance is a course of anti-depressant drugs – Largactyl for one, because the conventional wisdom is to be asleep.

So, here we are faced with the choice, wake up, and look at the universe, or close down, sleep and be a number.

I assume that those who decide to read on have also decided to wake up and have subscribed to the New Age conspiracy to embrace each other when they meet, irrespective of sex.

But there is a problem in the waking up, it's the loneliness if you do it by yourself. One has to look back into recorded history, as if one were sitting on the Moon and looking down on this planet, this heap of ants. Man's consciousness was tribal, and as Michael Bentine witnessed in the Amazonian jungles, a death in a tribe was known to other members at 20km distance, because they were part of the tribe in a real sense.

Western ego-consciousness has brought us all a load of agonies and glories, the glories of the supposedly crazy inventor – whether it's John Logie Baird showing a policeman in his garage how the television camera could work, or William Friese-Greene showing how the cinema could work. When Gutenberg first printed books with moveable type, cries of devilment were heard.

In the Eastern world there are scarcely any inventions by individuals. Indeed, there is scarcely any individuality, whether that is good or bad is open to interpretation, but it's a fact.

It was in the Western world when the "Age of Reason" took its grip that ego-consciousness grew up – the sense of being an individual – being prepared to be a maverick, an eccentric, an inventor, a top criminal even. That form of ego-consciousness which turns it's back on its group attachments, is part of the story.

When it takes the next step and moves to self-awareness, the psychological problems start. In 19th century romantic literature and poetry, struggled with a new reality of being is made manifestly clear.

From the "Age of Reason" two streams emerge, the Platonic and the Aristotelian. The Aristotelian world of the five senses reached its philosophical peak in the work of Karl Marx, in which man is held to be a socially engineerable Pavlovian electrochemical organism, and because it takes no account of the spiritual world, it is now going through a period of total revision.

The Platonic world of idea, the non-material, the spiritual, the subtle, is the stream that has succoured the New Age. But is a difficult world, because it isn't measurable by Aristotelian methods. You can't catch it, pin it down, measure it and file it away. It's a real challenge and a demanding world in which to become self-aware.

Sadly, most Western religious institutions have long ago renounced their spiritual heritage in favour of survival as institutions, committed to temporal affairs. The magic was lost. Some priests still understand the reality of spiritual science, but they are conspicuous by their paucity. I am grateful to count myself as a friend of some of them. Healing was one of the ministries given to the Apostles by Jesus. To heal within the church today is still held to be dubious, and not so long ago, to heal outside it was to be held to be in league with demonic powers. But I am happy to say that all is changing, and I personally have been made most welcome in many monasteries and convents in Western Europe to teach and demonstrate healing.

Anyway, we were talking about waking up, self-awareness, loneliness in the subtle world of consciousness, idea and spirit.

When you wake up, when you understand for the first time and you are you, alone in the universe, don't freak out and retreat into the world of material security and total boredom. Shake yourself as you look over the parapet, (once you have got over the shock,) and say, "Well, here I am. I know myself. What do I do next?"

The answer is to **learn to love.**

The French Symbolist movement was concerned with the Platonic world, and went in search of the Absolute, Nirvana, total being. They recognised there was a problem, and coined the expression, "crossing the abyss," which is a term used in magical ritual. You can make it a big deal, if you want to. It's as big or small as you care to make it.

What it means is once you've stuck your head above the parapet, and found no one's shooting at you, (except a few psychiatrists if you're unlucky enough to fall foul of them,) get up and cross no-man's land. The first steps maybe faltering then you begin to feel more secure. You walk upright with confidence, and suddenly you're over the abyss and it's a great transformation.

Paul Valery, the doyen of the symbolist movement once said about his search for the absolute, "Je me voyais me voir." – "I saw myself looking at myself." If you can tolerate that state, then you've made it, because you have discovered your essence, your soul, and from the soul point you can see your hyperself looking at your ordinary mundane self, warts and all, and that's knowledge. You've crossed the abyss from the mundane world to the world of spirit.

But knowledge is not enough. Love is the glue that makes it all hang together in a coherent whole. I mean of course pure love, not sentimental, dependent, conditional, self-seeking love, but that love which is total self-identification with the wholeness of the universe and which expects no rewards save the knowledge of self-completion. It's called Christian love by some, in other cultures it has other names, but it's the same thing at the end of the day. Indeed, once you have crossed the abyss it's not even difficult, it's so obvious a state to which to aspire that there is little more to be said.

I want to dwell a little on what has been said about loving oneself. It's all to do with knowing oneself. In the process of knowing oneself, we all find out things that we do not like. Don't worry about it. It's the same for everybody. We all have our murky corners. Strangely enough, it's only when we recognise them that we can be awake and when we do recognise them, it means we can do something about them.

At the end of the day, we may thus come to know our essential being and love it, because it's the divine spark that's within us all. If we can recognise it, and that's what we have to love. Indeed, we can't avoid it once we recognise it.

Right, we know ourselves, we've woken up, we're self-aware, we love ourselves, we love the whole universe, unsentimentally, but as self-identification. We are conscious at last, or as much as we may be.

Chapter 3

What is Consciousness

In a sense it's easier to say what consciousness is not. It is not simple brain function, not cerebral activity, nor simple mentation. The brain is an electro-chemical switching mechanism that relays messages around the body. Part of consciousness may include the brain, but it is an error to believe that the brain is the seat of the consciousness, and if consciousness isn't just thinking, what is it?

In the first instance it is structured. There are degrees of consciousness. As we said earlier, you can be more or less awake, or more or less self-aware, more or less conscious.

Some time ago, on BBC Radio 4, a senior physicist was asked whether consciousness was an objective field. He thought for a moment, then said it was a most interesting question, and he didn't know the answer. That is interesting, because a senior physicist is prepared to concede that ultimate reality is not necessarily Newtonian billiard ball mechanics, full of co-efficients and constants. For in order that consciousness may exist as an objective field, we are admitting that there are variables – what causes these variables, I will try to deal with that later.

First let me quote Sir James Jeans, Astronomer Royal in the 1930's, "The more I look at the Universe, the less it seems like a great machine, and the more it seems like a great idea." He would have been a Platonic. Eugene Wigner, companion of Einstein, stated in later life that the realisation that all things organic or inorganic has a spiritual essence had greatly contributed to his inner peace. Even Einstein, who after a discussion with Swami Tavore, (the Indian philosopher), said to him, "I am more religious than you."

There are many good quotes on my side. David Bohm for one or Werner Helensberg for another, who said that the behaviour of sub-atomic particles was in part conditioned by the observer, immediately qualifying reality as less than objective. Particle behaviour was probable, but not certain. Indeed, it has been suggested that in experimental apparatus such as exists at CERN, (Centre European de Recherche Nucleaire,) Geneva, certain sub-atomic particles appear to exist and function simply because they are posited as essential to the maintenance of a Newtonian vision of the universe. The idea of them exists, therefore they manifest.

Incidentally, I must point out that Newton was an esotericist, and the work he did in describing immediate reality as mechanistic is sadly taken by many to be his only contribution, the reverse is the case. Another who must be exonerated from his reputation is Descartes, supposed father of Cartesian reason. "Cognito, ergo sum." – "I think therefore I am," the opening words of "The Discourse Upon Reason." He was a Rosicrucian and esotericist. The Aristotelian of life have again used a small part of his work as if it were the whole to justify their case and, like Newton, he is vastly underestimated in respect of his true contribution.

A book I cannot recommend too highly is, "Mysticism and Modern Physics" by Michael Talbot.

The Age of Reason, that is to say the five sense world of Aristotle, produced a harvest of technological "goodies", blinding man to wider issues. That's why the planet is under ecological threat. It was cosily assumed that technology would solve all of man's problems. Indeed, it's only in the last 30 years that the notion of ecology as an amalgam of interacting natural forces has become popular, or even a concept. It only arose through the errors perpetrated by compartmentalising technology and over specialisation, creating a blinkered view of the planet.

It happens in medicine today. You can be shunted from one specialist to another and end up totally confused and abused. The true nature of reality is holistic, back to consciousness. Of course, words are difficult, vocabulary is inadequate. Indeed, scientists deliberately abuse words, using neo-classicisms, when most of the words they use are saying, "I don't know what this disease is."

For instance, "hepatitis" means a disease of the liver. The liver can have hundreds of different conditions, but if it can be labelled in a word stemming from Greek or Latin everyone feels a sense of relief. A label has been put on it, and a high- sounding label.

That is exactly the problem with consciousness and it's where I'm going to have to try terribly hard to be precise, although I know I can't be because of the problems of vocabulary.

Ludwig von Wittgenstein held the chair of philosophy in the 1930's at Cambridge and confused a generation of philosophy students by saying that words are not adequate to describe reality, thus producing a generation of nihilists. Before he died, he brought them back to reality by saying, "Of course, that is not to say that what is inexpressible does not exist."

Back to consciousness. Before even attempting to define it, let me say that it is the key to healing because it is the medium in which the idea has reality, thus it may have to do with the Greek notion of ether, the universal continuum. Actually, in spite of the drawbacks of vocabulary, that's not a bad effort!

The famous Michelson-Morley experiment to determine whether light was a particle or frequency is relevant. It was inconclusive, perhaps because it is both. In order for a frequency to exist, something has to vibrate. A particle is a theoretical solid which moves in various directions. Why shouldn't it be both? Electricity is a state of excitement of electrons. They vibrate, jump up and down. A frequency, which is beyond solids can, I submit, only exist if it has a medium to excite and therefore manifest itself. The contortions of Newtonian physicists to invent even more exotic particles, to keep the mechanical theory alive, is interesting to observe, thus the strange phenomena of CERN.

But you can't be the reductionist for ever. Frequency and wave forms take over. The problem then arises, that they must have a medium in which to oscillate.

As well as the Greeks, Eliphas Levi, the 19th century French esotericist, had something to say on the subject. "There exists an agent, at the same time natural and divine, material and spiritual, a plastic and universal medium, a common receptacle of vibrations and the images of form, a fluid and a force which may be to some extent called the imagination (or Idea) of Nature. The existence of this force constitutes the Great Arcanum of practical magic."

That's not a bad description of consciousness, given the fact that it's universal, transpersonal and not something unique to each individual. Because its structured, the higher states of consciousness are when we participate in universality, where the daily persona, the name on the driving licence, has no further relevance. It's the medium into which you wake up, (in the Gurdjieff sense), where you look around and feel alone. Unless you have learned the lesson of love, it is on the other side of the abyss, it is the world of spiritual sciences of Rudolph Steiner, it's the world where idea is reality, not solids, coefficients and constants. It's the world of God, for want of a better word, the Great Idea, and it is clearly beyond our means to understand why the world is imperfect, but at any rate we may be able to see that if we, as individuals, can participate by waking up in pure consciousness that is the universal continuum, we may, as Barry McWaters has well described in his book, "Conscious Evolution", or Sir George Trevelyan in "Operation Redemption", become co-creators with God, (that's not blasphemy,) and participate in the responsibility for the future evolution of consciousness in that neck of the universal woods which our planet represents.

Because consciousness is structured, the extent to which we wake up is the extent to which we aspire to participate in future evolution. The whole cycle of Western ego-consciousness and self-awareness, for all its technological glories, will only cross the abyss, as the automatic writings which guided Bligh Bond in his excavations of Glastonbury Abbey also say, when the evolved ego-consciousness returns to the collective consciousness in a voluntary act of self-surrender and pure love.

That is something that can only happen in the universal continuum and is why aspiring healers must wake up, look

13

around, love all things, and when they heal, participate in creating a new idea of the perfection of the person in front of them who is sick, or out of phase with their original hologram of perfection.

It's magic, it's spiritual science, it's participating in the action, it's self-fulfilment, it's what should be absolutely normal in the New Age.

UNLESS YOU WAKE UP, BECOME FULLY SELF AWARE, YOU CANNOT VISUALISE PROPERLY. ANOTHER KEY TO HEALING!

To return to consciousness and its structure. Part of the structure of consciousness is represented by what the Hindus call the chakras, the spinning wheels within all of us.

Chapter 4

Chakras, Consciousness and the Hologrammatic Nature of Reality

Traditionally, in Oriental lore, there have been seven chakras, (an excellent book on the subject is, "The Chakras", by C W Leadbeatter, of the Theosophical movement). The way in which a chakra may be defined, at least as far as the first seven are concerned, is that they represent energy centres which are outside the spectrum of positivist energies, and relate to the endocrine or glandular system.

In my experience, that would appear to be true, but they also connect with a subtle energy body beyond the etheric. They also represent aspects of consciousness. The ladder of the seven chakras, when it is fully awakened is the channel through which the Kundalini passes to illuminate the crown chakra and is nothing to do with the endocrine system. It is about waking up.

Of course, we are entering a multi-dimensional world where no one cause has only one effect. Thus, the two considerations may co-exist, and stimulating a chakra, through the healing process, may alleviate a weakness in the endocrine system. Having said the chakras also have to do with consciousness. Indeed, there is a substance known as serotonin which is released into the body when the agni (or third eye, or brow chakra,) is stimulated. It promotes higher consciousness and clairvoyance. One may say, therefore, that consciousness and the endocrine system are related, and that's demonstrable.

Consider adrenalin which accelerates the whole system, before races, before speeches, before virtually any important event. It is released in the blood stream when someone needs physically stimulation, and when this happens all the consciousness congregates around the base chakra. It also happens when someone gets into a violent mood, they get super energy from adrenalin.

Without describing the exact circumstances in which I have been able to dowse this phenomenon, as it's fairly difficult to say to someone in this state, "Do you mind? In the interests of knowledge, I'd like to dowse your base chakra!" I have achieved it twice. What happens is that the base chakra swells up draining the other chakras of energy'.

Whilst writing this book in Majorca, in circumstances which were obviously loving, rather than violent, Magdalena graciously consented to participate in an experiment which permitted me to observe on a more relaxed basis, that there is a reduction in the crown chakra in favour of the base chakra in certain non-violent circumstances. This demonstrates the nature of consciousness as a structured affair both in and outside the body. I would like to have pursued it further, but she couldn't stop laughing. However, the point was made, the two are related. Indeed, I have seen a photograph of a seer at San Damiano, where her auric saintliness, shows energy congregating around the crown chakra, and that is why religious pictures of the Middle Ages show the aureola or halo of the saint around the head. Remember this is not new knowledge. It is the same around the heart. What may be demonstrated is that when the

Greeks said that the heart was the seat of the emotions, they were right. Contemporary medical theory says the brain is all important, but healing and dowsing show that not to be the case. The brain is only a switching mechanism. When the energy of consciousness is around the head, it's only because that's the highest available point.

The emotions gather around the heart in a vast circle depending on their purity. It depends to what extent they are pure sentimentality or pure love. Now, if you want to be a saint, that's OK, but if you still want to walk down the high street in England, then sentiment will be a part of your life. The heart chakra when it is functioning well should be a perfect circle around the individual. It may extend to a radius of several metres, but a metre or so is OK for normal.

It should be continuous. If it only extends to the front and absent in the back, the healer knows the individual is suffering from an emotional trauma of the past. Making it whole again is part of healing. There may be just a segment missing, like a cheese triangle from the box, depending on the size of the trauma, but there is no pure health unless this chakra is uniform and circular. Differences in the extension of chakras, of course, explains why we feel comfortable or uncomfortable in the presence of different people.

The throat chakra may extend forward from the throat by up to 50 or 60 cm when people are particularly psychic though the normal is about 6cm. The stimulating of this chakra is a means of augmenting psychic perception and mediumship.

Of the other two chakras in the head, the crown chakra extends upwards exactly like a cone. It seems to be connected to cerebral activity and may be stimulated if someone is finding studying a bit difficult. Very often, when an individual has become hyperactive in that area, they will need help from a healer to reduce or close it down. Reducing activity in that area helps sleep.

The other chakra in the forehead, the brow chakra, projects forward, it can be up to some 50cm in length. This is also known as the magician's horn and, I believe, is the esoteric explanation of the unicorn as a mythical animal. Its adjustment is certainly best left to the individual, and its development depends on a highly evolved understanding of life by the individual who will adjust all their chakras at will anyway, on their own account.

The only other chakra I find in dowsing, is the solar plexus. It is our umbilical with the earth. Stimulating it slightly does seem to help people dowse the earth energies and it should, of course, always have some energy in it, but it is outside my experience to say whether it is ever necessary that it should extend more than a few inches.

Now, I hear you say! "There are more chakras than that. What about the sacral, and the sub chakras?" Particularly from clairvoyants, and "what about the colours"? Well, I love to work with clairvoyants, and I often have the sheer joy of working with people who can see physical bodies simply as energy forms. What a wonderful picture they paint! In some groups I've worked with, I've had up to three really good clairvoyants helping, all agreeing with each other as to what they see!

What I learned from this is that even though I feel with my hands, and they see clairvoyantly, we never ever disagreed in identifying problem areas. They might describe something as a black area. I would find it to be a hole in the etheric body. Or they might say, "The crown chakra is very dirty," where I would find parts of its natural symmetry missing and so on.

I will not, indeed I cannot say which approach is the most effective. I wish I was more clairvoyant – I do get flashes when I'm healing or just before doing a diagnosis, but I can't sustain it. I feel that I committed myself to the hands and that was it. Though as we'll see later, there are ways of stimulating clairvoyance through healing, I believe that the hands are the route for the rational healer.

What I find with the hands is different from the classical oriental version, as perceived clairvoyantly by C V Leadbeater. Again, it may well be that we are all talking about the same thing anyway, but as a multi-dimensional reality, a hologram.

Different means of perception may come up with differing versions of energy fields, but it's all the same thing in the end. In my case, basic vital energy manifests around people as a chequerboard.

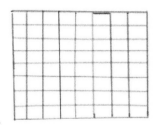

Thus:

8 X 8
8 X 16
8 X 32
8 X 64
Depending on the intensity.

A clairvoyant says. "Ah, now the fields are clean and vibrant," in a completely usual way. Whereas, for the rational healer, a physical person can be extrapolated in pure geometry, just as Pythagoras said. To the clairvoyant, the individual in good health is a symphony of light and colour.

It is the same thing and it's all in the hologram. It is not necessarily the best analogy, because it is in itself limiting, but it will do, for want of something better. It is now known that each of our cells contains the hologram of our being. So, I ask those who see chakras in different ways not to worry too much about my way of expressing them. We're all in the same business.

People talk about harmonising the chakras, as if it is a very complicated technical business. Later on, I will show that it's more straightforward than may appear at first sight.

How far have we progressed? May I just sum up?

An aspiring healer should wake up, become self-aware, understand the true nature of consciousness as the basic continuum of reality, understand the truth of pure love, learn to visualise with all his being and thus create a new idea of the perfection of the being who needs healing, and understand that individuals and cosmos are hologrammatic. In this way he is enabled to identify with cosmic consciousness, not to be terrified of being alone in the universe, (which is pure ego, not pure love.)

The more conscious we are, the more unsentimentally loving, we can be, the more we can penetrate the hologram, because consciousness is both local and infinite. Its higher form may be known as Christ Consciousness for that is how he healed, through the hologram.

I want now to go back to the beginning again, because I know people will be saying, "What's this dowsing business?" We understand the hologrammatic nature of being – what's dowsing got to do with it, and how do you use your hands to feel chakras, energy bodies, geometrical forms, etc.

Please treat this book as a hologram and not as a consecutive argument. The next chapter is about dowsing. It is crucial to the rational way to healing.

Chapter 5

Dowsing

The first thing about dowsing that springs to everyone's mind is water divining. Well, that works. It isn't a myth. I travel widely, and I know water diviners in at least 20 different countries, some of whom earn their living at it. The British Society of Dowsers has existed for over 50 years. The American Society of Dowsers, based in Vermont, has a long and honourable history. There are dowsing societies in most countries.

"Right!" you may say! That has been going since Moses, in spite of critical attitudes from the Church and State towards it. Maybe the Mosaical rods, as L rods used to be called in the 17th century, (because Moses called forth water in the desert?) or the diviner's Y-shaped hazel twig, or whalebone rods bound together at the one end, and the whole paraphernalia of gizmo's and gadgets that dowsers use are capable of picking up underground water. They bend, twitch, whirl, jump or coil, depending on the particular dowser's predilection for types of apparatus. They respond like antennae, picking up signals from underground water. Maybe because the human body is mostly water, we have some affinity towards it. Thus, we twitch when we're near it. Clearly, it works.

Well, that's the average reaction. I was the same... at the beginning.

The problem started when a friend of mine, Harold Wicks, who has a lot to answer for, changed my life, (without a Government Health Warning,) had me over for lunch one day. He lived then in the country near Tunbridge Wells.

"I've become a dowser," he said.

This was a critical point in my conversion. Had Harold been someone I hardly knew, I might have said something banal in rejoinder, but I had developed over the years a respectful appreciation of Harold's intellectual integrity. We had worked closely together in politics for some years and had come to trust each other's judgement. I certainly trusted him, and if he told me it worked, I immediately accepted it.

That was important. If any Tom, Dick or Harry said that to an unbeliever, he'd probably change the subject. Anyway, I showed interest and he explained to me, that a week or two before, across an adjacent field had come a strong smell of gas, on a Sunday so he called the Gas Board's emergency service. It wasn't long before he saw two men digging a hole in a nearby field. He went over to them, and indeed they were from the Gas Board and had found the fault. "That was quick," he observed. "Yes guv," one said, "We use the rods see!" holding up two L rods. "It's a lot quicker than using the official maps to find the pipe, and you can find the fault with them very quickly. Most of us use them." Now Harold accepted intellectually that they were describing a real phenomenon and thus his attitude to dowsing became, not whether it worked but how it worked?

So, he took up the rods himself and walked. He struck a pair in my hands. I couldn't get any reaction over his gas main at the first session. Then he took my hand in his and with a rod in his left hand and the other in my right hand, we tripped laughingly over his land.

"There you are," he said as his rod moved, Mine didn't. A few more tries. I started to try and make myself more aware of what he was feeling. Suddenly, our rods fired and I was away. I soon had his gas pipes, water mains, telephone cables and electrics all located. The rod had started to live in my hand.

"That's fun," I thought. Little did I know what I was getting into. (I have dropped others in it too, subsequently.) Even so, I still treated it as a new interest in life, rather than a huge new insight.

Little by little, as we met on later occasions, we played around with the phenomenon. One day, I remember, he came over to where I lived, and he decided to conduct a new experiment.

Each of us would go around the other side of the house and concentrate deliberately on a spot on the turf. The other would come around and try to identify the spot. It worked!

Which made it all the curiouser.

Subsequently, I was on a visit to my parent's home in Beckenham. My brother David, who lived with them, had become a dowser as well, and in a somewhat jocular vein, I offered to write a word on the lawn in the same way and see if he could dowse it. He'd got about half way through and looked up at me, (I was watching from an upstairs window,) and said. "I'd be obliged if you wouldn't write words like that on our lawn." But he laughed as he said it. Later on, he used to put pins in the lawn, and I would find them with the rods. It had all taken on a new dimension.

We then used the dowsing technique to investigate the whole ley line phenomena, in which we realised the true nature of the Holy Grail. An account can be found in the book, "Who'd Have Thought It", by Colin Bloy and Suzanne Thomas.

What we learned was that what was going on was not just a physiological reaction to water. The reasoning went as follows. It is not just water dowsing that works. You can dowse for gas mains, sewer pipes, electrical cables, telephone lines and so on. Not to mention words written on a lawn with the mind.

But if it's all just a psychological reaction to the external field, why doesn't a dowser in the High Street, in England not develop St Vitas Dance? The GPO dowser knows where his services are, and the gas board dowser can find the gas mains.

We studied the history of dowsing and found there were two basic schools, those who used a physical "witness", i.e. a sample of water, or coal, or oil for that matter. (there are hollow pendulums in which such witnesses may be inserted,) and those who don't use a physical witness. The former school claims that the pendulum or the rod is thus put into resonance with the "fundamental ray" of the substance they are looking for, but no one has been able to say that one school is more successful than another.

So, what's the difference?

In order to explain it, we had to formulate the idea of the mental witness. Instead of holding coal in your hand, you held it in your mind. You thought coal, and somehow that prevented you from being confused with water.

Conclusion. It's not a physiological phenomenon completely. It works according to what's going on in your mind – or your consciousness. When you think of the right thing, you find it, and when you don't, you don't. Thus, if the mind isn't concentrated, the rest doesn't work. You have to visualise what you are looking for. Thus, it's not a phenomenon like Galvani's frogs whose legs twitched when a current was passed through them. What is happening is that our brain is instructing our muscles to move and the rods to twitch.

Some years ago, the American Society of Dowsers ran an experiment with a group of people using rods over a field. Some were established dowsers, others interested but inexperienced, and the rest were off the street. The results were as you might expect. They were going over an underground stream, wired up to an electro-encephalograph. Whether their rods twitched or not, they all exhibited a shift in brain pattern of identical nature when they crossed the underground stream.

Thus, we concluded, dowsing is a phenomenon of the mind, not the body. The question is, how do we recognise the shift in the brain pattern when we cross underground water, or a gas pipe for that matter? Are we back to self-awareness, to waking up, are dowsers more awake than others? And if there is a shift in the brain pattern, with what does the dowser recognise it? The only conclusion we are able to come to, was with his consciousness.

Consciousness does not reside in the brain. The brain is the switching mechanism. Back to Paul Valery, "Je me voyais me voir." "I saw myself looking at myself." Which I is which?

Presumably part of that equation is the brain. With what is to be observed? It can only be through consciousness where the higher self-resides.

In order to dowse we have to be aware in our consciousness that our brain patterns change when we are dowsing. We also have to distinguish between the different signals of the different things we might be dowsing, and so by being dowsers, we are obliged to step aside conventional "consciousness" or "brain consciousness" in order for the dowsing experience to work.

This is only the start. What on earth can we make of map dowsing? It really puzzled me in the beginning. That someone can take a map of a place he has never visited, hold a pendulum over it and indicate where the water, land drains or whatever it might be.

At the beginning, I couldn't really get on with the pendulum. Then one day, for reasons told elsewhere, ("Who'd Have Thought It"), a wise old Welsh wizard, Bill Lewis, took my aura into his. He had a spring-loaded gizmo in his hand which he twirled in order to do it. I felt a tingling in my hand. Dylan a clairvoyant watched it happening, then confirmed that my aura had gone. Then Bill put it back, twirling the other way.

I can only assume that there is such a thing as auric communication, or perhaps he slipped me a bit of his. In any event, from that day on the pendulum lived in my hand, and I could map dowse, although I only used it to dowse ley-lines.

One day, some years later, again with Harold, we went out together in the car to try and locate the great St Michael energy line that runs from St Michael's Mount in Cornwall to Bury St Edmunds in Suffolk. He drove, and I spread the maps on my knees, pointing with a fore finger and holding the pendulum in the other hand.

"You're on it now," he suddenly said as he drove on.

27

"What do you mean?"

"Your fingers on it now. I felt a sort of spark between us."

He was right.

That set me thinking some more. Not only could I map-dowse, but Harold could map dowse through me! Curiouser and curiouser!

Colin Wilson tells in one of his books, "Mysteries", of his experiences with Robert Leftwich, dowser of Sussex. Not only did he dowse water on land but if he sent someone else walking over the land, whilst he remained behind, seated, holding a rod, he could tell when that person was over water. "Ho, ho," I thought. "That means you can send your servant out to do the leg-work!"

Just the other day, in Majorca, some 30 members of Fountain International went on a coach trip to dowse the energies of the monastery of Lluch, where Raimond Llull, a knowledgeable 12th century monk, spent much time. The coach driver, drove up the mountain on precipitous roads, (happily called Gabriel), noticed the dowsing rods and was intrigued.

"My wife does that," he said. "She has just found water on some land we bought. 7,000 litres and hour at 90 metres. Cost me a million pesetas, (£5,000) to drill it, but it was worth it.

He then went on to recall that he was talking about this to a friend, who asked him to scratch in the sand with a stick a rough map of the property. He got out his pendulum, indicating precisely where Gabriel's wife had found water.

So, we have come a long way from seeing dowsing as merely a physiological reaction to an external objective field. It is a phenomenon of consciousness, of self-awareness, of being able to visualise what we are looking for, and being able to observe our own brain rhythms.

In a paper published by the British Society of Dowsers, some work was done on one of Maxwell Cade's Mind Mirrors. This is a sophisticated form of EEG, two in parallel, measuring left and right hemispheres of the brain. There is a reason to believe that what we might call intuition operates in the right hemisphere, and the left contains the rational mind. The output of the EEG's is fed into a series of fibre optic bulbs which permits a sine wave to develop according to which lights are lit. One of the conclusions was that the state of the brain rhythm of the dowser was very like that obtained from someone in a state of Zen meditation, which in esoteric circles is a very advanced state.

It's quicker to learn to dowse than to practice meditation which is useful to know.

But what I conclude from all of this is that the dowsing state is a way of tuning in to the universal consciousness, the world of "idea". By "idea", I don't mean "idea" in its conventional sense, but in the sense of the ultimate in non-material terms of the reality of a person or thing.

Once we can use our consciousness in this way, we are well down the rational path to spiritual healing.

This is not a criticism of meditation. It is a way, but it is in my opinion cumbersome, lengthy, and sometimes misleading. If you can learn to dowse, I believe that it is a short-cut.

Chapter 6

The Reality of Spiritual Fields

After looking through theoretical concepts, let us now get down to business.

The first exercise is to rub the palms of your hands together vigorously. It's not essential, but if you are a beginner, it does seem to stimulate the sensitivity of your hands. Stretch out the arms as far as they will go, and tell yourself, I'm feeling nothing. Which is not that difficult.

Now start to bring the palms of the hands together from a distance, remembering that you are coming from nothing to something, so there may well be a difference in your sensation. It depends on your own energy field as to the distance at which the change occurs. It might be 6 cm, it might be 20cm. It could be further than your arms reach, but that's a bit special, but as your hands start to get between 10-20 cm apart, you may well find, (if your mind is relaxed so that the higher you is looking at your brain), that there is a sensation just like the opposing poles of a magnet repelling each other, a form of pressure. With some, it might just be like ants tickling the palms, with others heat or cold, it doesn't matter. Each to their own.

What does matter is that the sensation, whatever it is, is consistent.

Try now, to see if you can find out what is yours. Most people seem to find pressure is their particular sensation.

The question arises as to whether or not it is a physiological sensation. In my experience it certainly feels like it is. To me it seems we are dowsing with the palms of our hands. Because this sensation may be used to identify up to 16 different energy bodies of individuals, we have to create different forms of witness in our consciousness in order to recognise the difference. That's when the sensation only occurs at our conscious request.

You say to yourself, "I want to look at the third body." Thus, the sensation occurs in conformity with the configuration of the energy body. I intend to describe the different energy bodies in this hologrammatic narrative when the right point occurs.

We must determine what we are looking at in our consciousness in order to regulate the correct sensory feedback.

With a bit of practice and acceptance that all this is not some form of illusion or confidence trick, most people can get it. If you've already got to water, pipes or energy line dowsing, this jump will be an easy one, so let's not devote too much time to it.

But it is the rational way to healing. Because if you can feel an aura, or etheric body, (the first energy body), then you can feel those people in front of you who need healing, and you too, can go down to the pub, do a few miracles and be back in time for lunch.

In case you dismiss that as sounding too flippant, I would like to say here and now before I try to expatiate the theme in some detail later on, that we are dealing with the sacred, the responsible, the loving, the divine – but we are not dealing with the sombre, the Sabbatarian, the gloom of worthiness, the misery of all dedicated virtue. We are dealing with the joy of living and giving, of communicating, of the happiness of sharing with an open heart. In that business, you are allowed a laugh or two, a happy smile and a giggle. It actually doesn't work if you take it too seriously. That's why good healers laugh a lot.

If by now you can feel the first energy body of your own body, (which may extend some 12cm around the physical body, in a normal healthy person,) you can try to apply the technique to others. You will soon be able to tell if a person is in good or bad general health by simply running your hand at a distance around them. Indeed, simply boosting that basic energy field, in itself can correct many negative conditions. In due course I will explain how to boost it. This book is a hologram and must come to the central point from all directions.

Once we have got that simple sensation of feeling the etheric or first energy body around a person, we can start to learn about the health problems of that person, if they have any. If there is no sensation, then that person is either in, or on the way to ill health. You may have to boost the field in order to find out in which points of the body the energy is lacking.

I will discuss some of the conclusions that one may make from observation of this field.

If the field is uniform all over, that's a good sign. Where however, a particular organ is not well, then around that organ will be no energy, or reduced energy. The illness may not yet be manifest to the person but there is a potential problem if it can be observed in the etheric body or aura.

A healer may observe the first and most important, but least dramatic of all the duties of the healer, which is.

Miracles shall not be necessary

There is a danger amongst incipient healers that they will feel that healing is miracles or nothing. In fact, it's the opposite.

It is sad that the healer today is often the last recourse. Indeed, when certain comparisons of results are made, this should be borne in mind. Only too often healers have to deal with the hopeless, the abandoned, the impossible. This is beginning to change, thank God, because of a dawning awareness that healing can be preventative, but it has not always been the case.

The pursuit of the miraculous is something that healers should abjure, unless there is no other option. At all costs the healer should avoid feeling that it's a miracle or nothing. I do know a few people who hope that hopeless cases will be sent to them so that they may demonstrate their powers. That is the road to self-delusion. Good healing is simply giving a person good health undramatically. I hope one day it will be such a matter of routine between ordinary folk, that the role of the healer in society as a special person will disappear.

The simple things about healing that are the most important, keeping a person well is much more significant than miraculously reversing cancer. I have done that. At least, some say I have. Of course, I know I've had the privilege of doing it, of being a channel. Not always, but often.

Ask Tito, the tailor in Salamanca, who was opened up, and when the surgeon saw the extent of the abdominal cancer, he closed him up again and said that there was nothing to be done. He's fit and well today, and the latest scan showed he had nothing any more, November 1987.

When you think about it, it would have been far better to have given him healing years ago, so he never contracted the cancer. Healers must beware of glory and only accept it reluctantly.

Tito recognised the benefits of healing, and he now permits his tailors' workshop to be used as a healing centre in Salamanca.

As a matter of interest, his cancer was healed simply by augmenting his basic energy field. Everybody does not yield to this treatment, and later I'll try to deal with the causes of more difficult cancers, which frequently are the result of a desire to die.

If the etheric body is uniform, then things are generally fine. If there are holes in it, and the hand will touch the physical body at those points because there is no resistance, it gives us a very important clue as to where a person maybe ill or potentially ill. Simply putting that energy field together again is very important, but meanwhile it helps us to identify where we should perhaps do what is known, misleadingly, as a "psychic operation".

If the field attenuates at the extremities of the arms or legs, an indication of the existence of rheumatism, arthritis, bad circulation and so on putting it right generally helps these conditions.

Working with acupuncturists in Europe and China, it seemed possible to demonstrate that spiritual healing stimulates the energy meridians of acupuncture and thus may be seen, at this level, to be a form of acupuncture without needles or even touching the person.

Acupuncturists are sensitive to several pulses in the wrist and have confirmed that spiritual healing, like their needles, does change the meridians.

One may ask, of course, to what extent a knowledge of anatomy is essential? It is never bad, but it is not essential at this stage of healing. A hole in the energy body is a hole, its causes may be outside the normal terms of reference of conventional medicine and just putting it right may be all that is necessary.

An important feature of the etheric body is the way it also is cut when the physical body undergoes a surgical operation. It is in my experience, very helpful if a healer prepares someone before an operation, boosting up their basic energy field, and gets to them immediately afterwards to repair the damage done to the etheric, the physical healing processes of the body are stimulated, resistance to post-operational shock is increased, convalescence is much speedier.

My sister, had to have a hip operation some years ago, and I worked with her like that. We did not tell the surgeon, and he was amazed at her recovery, she left hospital several days earlier than normal in these cases. It seems clear to me that one way to make the NHS more efficient is to use healers in this way.

In a hospital in Madrid, the theatre sisters, who had been to one of our courses, employed healing in this way and reported to me a 38% increase in efficiency of their wards and theatres.

I would hope one day that spiritual healing at this level would be part and parcel of general nursing, not to mention surgery itself.

Although I've lost touch with him now, I once taught a Spanish surgeon how to heal whilst operating. He then landed a top position in Houston, Texas, so I never heard how it worked out, but the theory seems good. There are not too many surgeons I know who would be prepared to work this way, but I'm sure it will come.

I cannot support certain fanatical healers who wish to ban orthodox medicine and will have nothing to do with doctors, or patients who are undergoing medical treatment. It's absurd to deny anyone the benefits of spiritual healing simply because they are taking medication. Someone on chemotherapy needs healing more than anyone else. Healing helps the person take from medication what is genuinely helpful to them, resisting the negative side effects.

For the foreseeable future, orthodox medicine and healing should go hand in hand. Together they can improve health care enormously, along with other complementary therapies.

The first thing a healer must do is to develop authority and confidence, in order to enlist the most powerful weapon in the healing arts, the power of suggestion.

I remember once having to go to a GP's surgery for a prescription for one of my children on Christmas Eve, and I groaned at the thought of waiting in an enormous queue.

To my surprise, there was nobody in the surgery, and the doctor was reading the paper.

"What's the matter," I said. "Have you finally managed to kill off all your patients?" "Didn't you know?" he replied. "Nobody gets ill over Christmas if they can help it."

That was a powerful comment on the nature of illness. I suppose if we can make Christmas Day every day, a lot of illness would disappear? Happy people have less illness, than unhappy people. Some people want to be ill, they actually enjoy bad health.

I know someone, who has spent more time in doctor's surgeries for obscure and vague reasons than doing something constructive with their life. This person devotes a great deal of mental energy into worrying about health, planning a week of visits to the GP, the neurologist, having a blood test, and so on. It is sad to watch, sad to see so much time wasted in such negative pursuits.

The point of all this is that the power of suggestion is tremendously important to any doctor, healer or therapist. It's been suggested that most illnesses heal themselves, no matter what the doctors may do, and of course the placebo effect is well-known.

What may be less well-known, is that in a series of tests in the US with placebo and the real thing, it became evident that a certain percentage of the doctors were getting consistently good results, with the placebo or with the drug, and what's more, even when they didn't know which their patient was taking. That is important. It indicates that a certain type of individual gets good results because of something in him, his style perhaps, his authority, his presence, his charisma?

It may be that certain doctors have a greater capacity to use suggestion than others. When Jesus said to a cripple, "Take up they bed and walk," this defied argument. One can hear the beggar saying, "Of course Lord. Right away Lord. Can't think why I didn't do it before! Terribly sorry Lord!" and walking away happily. That was a great healing, but it relied heavily in the power of suggestion, and no healers should ever dismiss it from his armoury.

As my dear friend and great healer, John Leslie, once said. "I don't care how I do it. I'll put on a straw hat and do a dance, if that will do the trick. It's the result that counts." Of course, John did perform great and dramatic psychic operations, but not just because it was good for his ego, only when it was necessary.

We must be careful, therefore, not to fall into the trap of thinking we must always go into an elaborate healing, when perhaps a good mental kick in the backside is what is necessary, or perhaps LOVE. Some people become ill for lack of love, some people stay ill for the lack of love, and some people die for the lack of love. Some people go to the doctor because they have nowhere else to go.

This is the sphere where the increasing institutionalisation of medical services is actually contributing to bad public health and increasing its work load. Maybe those doctors who healed better regardless of drug or placebo, did so because they loved their patients more? Was their attitude to the person for whom they were prescribing different?

To appear on an army sick parade is quite an experience, usually the Regimental Sergeant Major assumes you are swinging the lead. I was on one once during National Service. "What's the matter with you then soldier?" "Acute anal irritation," was my reply. He went puce and threatened to put me on a charge. Then you are marched in front of the Medical Officer and come to attention, bang, bang, salute, and wait for him to speak to you.

I told him. He didn't look up. "Zinc ointment," he said to the orderly. "Return to duty, soldier."

It cleared up. Perhaps the fear of the system was the trigger. I supposed you can be too frightened to be ill, as well as too happy.

There are now computers with which the sick people may talk and discuss their symptoms. The computer then prescribes. The computer manufacturers say it's all much better because people are less embarrassed talking to a computer than a real live doctor. I wonder?

Is there not a factor which manifests in the relationship between doctor and patient which may be positive, which needs a little more time spent on each case for it to develop, rather than, "a No 9 pill, a dose of jollop, and next please!"

I am sure all good doctors know this, but increasing bureaucratisation of medicine conspires to eliminate this factor.

No healer should ever ignore it. We should approach everyone with authority, confidence and love. I don't mean reckless authority – of course I can heal you, but the quiet authority of, you know I will do my best for you. Healing works. It may help you, and eye to eye contact. Let them talk about themselves. Create a friendly atmosphere. It's all part of healing.

The BMA's report on Complementary Medicine although I feel is superficial, and written to suit a prior attitude, did say that alternative practitioners do get better results in some cases because of the time spent with their patients. Well, that's important.

Some time ago the medical profession in Britain said in a report something to the effect that it felt that some 80% of illness, which is not due to accident or infection, was psychosomatic in origin. This seems to be a very fundamental observation about the nature of disease.

The question remains as to how you heal psychosomatically. Should all doctors be psychiatrists? There is little doubt that much illness is self-healing, that the body has its own powers of recuperation. The question is how do you trigger it off?

What I am trying to say to an aspiring healer is that if you can feel a person's basic energy field, know where and how to boost it, and be prepared to spend time with the individual, you are already equipped to do an awful lot of good. Some of it will simple be revitalising the whole organism energetically, and some of it will be by triggering off self-healing psychologically, some of it will be simply by giving love!

You may ask, "If I can feel the energy fields and know where I need to boost them, how do I do that?

Chapter 7

Giving Vital Energy

I go back to the concept of consciousness as an objective and universal field, and the model of reality as idea rather than substance.

When we are in a state of higher awareness attainable by dowsing and we are aware of our higher self-observing our lower selves, then we can create, through visualisation, new ideas, not conceive them, but create them. And we may, through the universal continuum of pure consciousness, transmit these ideas anywhere in the universe not just to the person in front.

When we began to dowse ley lines and show that an objective energy runs along them (many ley lines involve modern centres, not just ancient ones), we also found that ephemeral energy lines could come into being, especially where some sort of spiritual activity was going on. An aware and sincere priest and congregation produce more powerful energies in and around the church and local ley lines during the service.

It has been found that similar energy lines came in and out of the sanctuaries that many healers keep in their homes for their work. When outside their sanctuaries, or in a ploughed field for that matter, they instinctively plugged into the permanent node points in the ley-system, not necessarily the nearest, but those which permit the most symmetrical form, a cross of energy lines, to form on the healer himself, thus ley lines work by the number of parallels in the lines. This may increase the intensity at which the healer works.

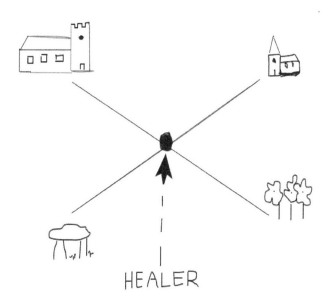

HEALER

It may also be found through dowsing, that a vertical column of energy forms around the healer. It is palpable, measurable, visible to some and photographable.

My experience of this energy and how it works, plus an understanding of the Gospels and the Acts of the Apostles, leads me to believe that this energy is what is referred to as the Holy Spirit. In other religio-cultural systems it may occur as Prana, Mana, the Primum Mobile of Alchemy, etc. It is not a unique Christian phenomenon.

You may, in the dowsing state, put your arms around it and feel its circumference. If you go inside it, you will find it is made up of concentric circles. If you have the vision, you may see that each circle is a different colour. The circles multiply according to intensity and thus may be counted or measured. This energy can be photographed in some detail. It's not all that difficult, and I will expand on this later.

You may remember I spoke about Maxwell Cade and his Mind Mirror earlier. It wasn't used only to measure the brain waves of dowsers and high-class meditators, it was used on healers as well. Nina Coxhead wrote a book, "The Powers of the Mind," about Cade's work and she told how healers patterns change when they heal, moving into what may be called a purer state of consciousness. It is fascinating that after a while the brain pattern of the sick person starts to take on the same rhythm. What is even more fascinating is that a sick person being treated by a healer some distance away, say in another room, starts to take on that pattern as well. The division of brain rhythms into Alpha, Beta, Gamma, Delta etc is a useful yard-stick. Healing and dowsing do seem to include a lot of Alpha and other things as well. It's a bit more complex than it seems. The rhythm, I believe, is not the state itself, but an indication from the brain that the consciousness it serves is changing from the normal. Actually, some people appear to be in Alpha all day long. That may be the path to sainthood!

At this point I recommend very highly the Jose Silva's "Mind Control" courses, which are excellent in teaching you how to understand mind, brain and consciousness and how to open the door to healing in a rational way. They are expensive, totally ethical, thorough and do not seek to trap you into a sect. I know many healers in Spain who have come out of the Silva courses, and the most sectarian thing they have become involved with is an association of Silva graduates who practice healing.

The Mind Mirror appears to be saying that the consciousness of both healer and sick person changes, becoming identical.

May I add two further observations from my own experience as a dowser. When a healer heals, not only is he plugged into the ley system, and the vertical column, which I prefer to call cosmic consciousness or Holy Spirit, but when you dowse his own personal fields with the hand the energy disappears. So, does the sick person's, at least from the back each person. You feel nothing. But between them from the forehead to the feet is a field that, as it were, joins them in one single energy body. It's not apparently structured, chakras, etc, but it occurs at the same time as the two brain rhythms combine.

Secondly, a healer working at a distance emits his own energy line, just like a ley line, to the sick person at whatever distance.

I have been in France with a sick person when a group of English healers has gone to work on him, and from the direction of England came a powerful energy line. I have also been in Spain when a group was not sure of the precise location of the person. The energy line found its way there without any trouble.

It's also notable that when a healer goes into the actual act of healing, the vertical column becomes very narrow, the size of the top of the head, and instead of being around him enters at the point of the crown chakra.

When healers do not get into this narrow focus, they seem to exhaust themselves very quickly. To ensure the narrow focus by visualisation permits a healer to work an eight-hour day like anyone else, because it's not your energy you are giving. It is very important. A healer is a channel, not a source. It's a privilege, but we must never fall into the ego trap of believing it is ourselves. Of course, we need not be so humble as to disclaim all responsibility. We do have to perform well as channels, but healing is divine. We are acting as a servant, however good a servant we may be.

I hope by now I have said enough on the subject to offer the concept of healing as being a spiritual science, an empirical, demonstrable, repeatable system of disciplines and exercises, which may employ scientific method just as the material sciences.

The problem about repetitive phenomena in identical conditions, the test applied by the material scientist for the acceptance of new data, is not so much the repetition, but that the existence of identical conditions is not determinable by positivist scientific methods.

You would have to test for brain rhythm, state of consciousness and subtle energy fields from outside, from the observers. Some physiological monitoring is available on a positivist basis, but one cannot expect the apparatus of positivism to be able to detect subtle phenomena that by the nature of its definition of itself, says it cannot exist.

As Michael Bentine, often says. "If you ask the electricity man to measure a gas main with a voltmeter, you can hardly be surprised if he is incapable of drawing conclusions."

So that's the problem, although many modern physicists are accepting a metaphysical model of reality which does not accept the subtle, ephemeral, relative, even spiritual with its system. From this may well flow a more positive attitude to the subtle world of the spirit from "positivist."

There are exercises, techniques and apparatus available to help along the road. One may use bio-feedback. This is equipment which will tell you when you are in Alpha rhythm. You can soon learn the trick of seeing yourself watching yourself, and of course, there's the dowsing route. It is all part of heightened awareness.

Once you have determined that the sick person at least needs a general boost, put yourself into an Alpha state. Get rid of all the extraneous chatter and the daily personality, it's irrelevant now, and concentrate solely on the job in hand. Identify totally with the sick person.

Visualise! That is to say, "See in your inner being the four lines coming in on you from the ley system." Plug in. Ask for the column of light to come down upon you. Put it into narrow focus in your crown chakra. This will soon become an automatic discipline that you can flip in an instant. Above all, say, "God, please help me to do this correctly." It helps get things into perspective, and it is not blasphemous to say the Holy Spirit is intelligent. Very often you may find healings occur without your understanding. As I said before, healing is a sacred science. It requires our constant reverence, love and the right degree of humility, combined with certainty confidence and total self-control. This is not to detract in any way from trance healers. They are often, acting as a channel for discarnate beings to act through them, and can be highly effective.

In this state of heightened awareness start to visualise, to build in your consciousness the idea of the sick person re-vitalised, and transmit that idea to the person. Consciously draw in the vital energy from the ley system, and draw down the column of light the cosmic energy. Mix it in the solar plexus chakra and then visualise it passing through the arms to the sick person, because visualisation causes the energy to run. The creation of the idea in the continuum of consciousness is the trigger that produces a measurable result. You will feel the result with your hands when you have finished.

Do you need to lay hands on a person? Technically not, but I always feel that human touch is psychologically important. It creates human warmth, it helps to create the suggestion and if one healed simply by saying nothing and looking at the person, omitting energy through the eyes, a lot of people would feel cheated, mystified, and may indeed put themselves into a negative state which is non-receptive.

Often, they will say that they feel intense heat coming from the hands of the healer.

Where should we lay hands? Again, it doesn't matter too much. It may be on top of the head, on the shoulders. I find I like to stand sideways onto the person, putting a hand just below the solar plexus and the other, the right hand, in the small of the back.

The solar plexus is the part in the energy body the Oriental's call the HARA, the epicentre, the pivotal point, and I do feel that whatever we do, that's were vital energy enters the system anyway, so one might as well put one's hands there in the first place. As you do it, visualise it running through the whole organism of the sick person, see every organ throbbing with new life, the nervous system functioning efficiently, with healthy blood running smoothly around the body- go on, give it to them! And anything else you can think of. Perfect the idea of the person in mind body and spirit.

What is the difference between cosmic energy and ley energy? Cosmic energy, as I said earlier, is the Holy Spirit, Mana, Prana, whatever. When it is photographed it appears white. It's essential to healing, for it is that within which we make new ideas.

Ley energy may also be held to be earth energy, the basic vital energy of our globe that comes spiralling out of certain parts of the earth, tree circles, springs, earth faults, head of valleys, certain earth temples deliberately constructed by man. There are many on the chalk downs in Sussex and Kent, because the soft rolling downs don't have sharp enough clefts for the dragon to get out. Stone-Age man understood both these energies, and his monuments show it.

The spiral earth energy is the basis of all dragon myths in all cultures. It certainly is in China, and they refer specifically to ley lines as dragon lines and certain types of mountain formation as azure dragons, from which energy comes. I have had the pleasure of dowsing around the Ming tombs near Peking, which are organised in this way quite specifically.

The Chinese placate their dragons, they think if properly treated they bring good fortune and health.

In the West, we treat our dragons badly. We kill them. However, I believe this is a Christian ecclesiastical overlay to hide a truth of pre-Christian religion. Our dragons are held to be evil, and indeed in some Christian myth represent Pagan religion itself.

When Christianity moved in as the state religion of Imperial Rome, many things were changed to suit the needs of the state. The Council of Nicaea in 325AD was held at the diktat of Constantine, and the Christian bishops clearly told what the state required of them. Thus, four gospels out of some thirty were decided to be canonical, parts of them obviously doctored, and Christianity became Romanised.

This state religion, therefore became an institution, and all human institutions tend to place their own survival higher than the truth they originally represented. Thus, the joys of early Christianity were lost, the Church hierarchy was formalised, and lay people were excluded from talking to God and the angels on their own account. It could only be done, from that time on, through the intermediary of the priesthood. This gives more political control.

Whereas early Christianity had no difficulty, indeed was welcomed by the natural religions of the Celts, it became a matter of state policy to exclude the laity from all direct contact with the subtle.

Thus, dragons had to be changed. Instead of a swirling vortex of vital fiery energy waiting to be channelled constructively through the rod of higher consciousness into individuals and communities. Christian saints, angels and archangels were held to kill dragons stone-dead with their spears and swords. It was symbolic of destroying the heathen religion, and appears in this way in Christian iconography.

In fact, the dragon really is the raw vertical spiral energy of the earth. Dowsers will find it as a spiral in these places, and in most cases, the spiral straightens out into a ley line and enters the community in a vitalising way. But it is put into a constructive mode by the hyperconsciousness of man.

Healers plug into the ley-system, (which is the structured form of dragon energy), draw it in from the earth and give it further structure by mixing it with cosmic energy, and the two act as the vehicle for the transmission of a new idea of health to a sick person.

I saw the true nature of this in a photograph of the clairvoyant lady of San Damiano, Italy, who had the visions of the Virgin Mary. The dark earth energy was entering the lower part of her body, and the white cosmic energy was illuminating the crown chakra, streaming backwards as the lady walked along. If she had been stationary the cosmic energy, I believe, would have been vertical. Also, on the photo, I was able to discern two white energy "wings" emerging from her shoulders. These energy wings appear on people, and may be felt, in the dowsing mode with the hands. What they indicate is that you are in what may be termed the saintly state, and the energy of the heart chakra, which is the seat of the sentiments, is transmuted upwards to produce these wings.

However pure the sentiment or emotions may be, certain healers may not be capable of pure love for certain people. They tend to be selective, whereas true love from the spirit is even handed. True spiritual love is unsentimental. That may sound a bit cold, but it is true. It's one of the reasons healers have difficulty in healing people close to them, particularly wives and sweethearts, blood relatives and so on. The sentimental attachment we have for such people prevents us from even handedness that creates that dissociation in higher consciousness which permits the greater clarity in visualisation. It's often better to send your loved ones to other healers you trust.

I really do get the best results with people I've never met before. I have no emotional complications with them. Thus, I can be totally objective.

John Leslie always replied when somebody asked him whether their healing would be successful. "What's done, is done," which would leave some mystified. What he meant was that a healing, for best results, should be a self-contained integral act. Once it was over, that was it. It shouldn't even be discussed on a questioning basis.

You should not pick at it. "I wonder if that person was healed. Wouldn't it be nice if they got better." If you have done your job properly, then there is no more you can do, and it's an old rule in spiritual science, not to discuss an operation or even think about it, lest you start to unpick the warp and weft of the idea you have created in pure consciousness.

Get on with the next one. Do not worry whether it worked or not. "What's done is done." The more we dissociate, the more effectively we can work. That's why the expression "sub rose" exists.

Once you have mastered the foregoing, you are a spiritual healer. There really is a lot of good you can do simply at that level. In Salamanca, in one treatment, just by boosting the person's general energy field, a young man who had been in a wheelchair for two years after an accident was walking within a week, with no further pain. So, you need not necessarily go into the rest of this business to perform useful things for people, but I hope you do read on, because now it really starts to become quite technical, and more fascinating.

Chapter 8

Dowsing and Interpreting Chakras

We saw how a healthy person always has a continuous field around the body of some six inches. It can vary. Now in order to feel the chakras, one must switch the mode in the consciousness from visualising basic vital energy to looking for chakras. They are on a different vibrational level to basic energy.

That having been done, you should now be able at certain points to feel the extent or lack of it around the body. An ideal state for someone is shown below.

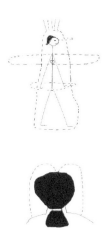

We discussed the nature of chakras earlier. In my experience, depression may be quickly spotted by the crown chakra's nonexistence and a form of cork in the top if the head, as on previous page.

Restoring the crown chakra re-invigorates the person spiritually and is the start of creating inner peace. Depression just does not help illness, it only makes it worse. Once again, that straightforward act of healing can often get what's wrong right.

Experience indicates that this chakra needs to be in balance with the heart chakra, which should be a circle about three feet in radius around the heart area. It is the seat of the sentiments, just as the Greek said, not the brain.

A person in a loving state may have a heart chakra with a radius of three or four yards, but three feet is a good average. If you are in love, that chakra is big. But you can be in love with humanity, as opposed to one human being, or anything else. If it's non-existent it is an indication that the individual may be bitter, emotionally shocked, traumatised. Similarly, if the back part or a segment of the chakra is missing. Restoring it frequently gets rid of the trauma and other symptoms clear up rapidly.

I believe many skin conditions are caused by emotional problems. I recall many cases of eczema, psoriasis, and sadly healers tend to get the worse cases, some quite alarming disfigurations of the skin, amounting to a most reptilian appearance. In these cases, repeated treatment and also light suggestion in a relaxed state listening to music has produced the right result. The cause apparently emotional distress, but suggestion must have helped as well.

If there is not emotional and spiritual harmony, then the weak points of the body, (and we all have them), will start to give trouble. Once again it is relatively simple to give relief and remedy.

The throat chakra which extends forward, rather than around the throat. Where there are thyroid problems, this chakra will seem weak and boosting it will often do the trick. Extending it too far, more than three or four inches has the effect of increasing psychism, which may be desirable in one but not in inexperienced people. Such boosting should only be done in close consultation with the person concerned, who must understand what's happening.

The brow chakra may extend up to two feet when the brain is very active, and if one is studying for exams this may be useful. A healer can help develop concentration by boosting this chakra. On the other hand, we all know we sometimes get into a rut. We can't stop the brain, can't sleep at night, and the recipe for a nervous breakdown (whatever that is) exists. Reducing that chakra calms the mind, enables normal sleep patterns to return, and generally alleviates stress.

The magician's horn is not, I believe, as I said before, for healers to deal with. It is for evolved practitioners of meditation to deal with on their own account.

As to the solar plexus chakra, I can only say that it appears right that it should not extend more than a few inches, but stimulating it a bit does seem to help dowsing

Later, I will explain a method for creating harmony between all chakras, but it involves explaining another dimension of healing first.

How may chakras be boosted or reduced? In the same manner as giving vital energy. Visualisation. I find it useful to use the hands, and its rather like strands of pastry sticking to them and spreading them out when required. It is in the world of imagination where we must first create that idea in our own consciousness, in order to communicate it and achieve the affect.

One further point, where someone is very depleted, you have first to restore the basic energy in order to be able to assess the state of the chakras, so one must always look at the etheric body first.

There are also a number of situations in which the whole etheric body and chakra system will be found to be out of the perpendicular, projecting forward at an angle of some five to thirty degrees downwards from the head, and entirely separated by the time you have got down to the feet.

This is usually due to violent shock, emotional or physical, a whiplash in a car accident for example, or the sudden death of a loved one, a dramatic withdrawal of affection in a love affair. The symptoms are usually described as a sensation of feeling two people, being outside oneself, of general disorientation. It can produce all sorts of vague unspecified symptoms. The onset of puberty as well is a shock which can produce this effect in adolescents, also in menopause.

Strangely enough, this is one of the easiest conditions to correct and usually has instant results. Doing the visualisation and pointing with the finger, starting at the top of the head, and from the side you move down, visualising all the while that the etheric body is coming into perpendicular with the physical. It's as well to do it front ways on as well. The result is immediate. Of course, it's a sign of the cross. Is this what a blessing really was?

Putting the etheric body and chakras right before and after operations, and during any therapy, is a very helpful contribution the healer may make to orthodox medicine.

Chapter 9

Using the Fingertips

Dowsing the fields with the hands is useful, but when one stops and thinks, there may well be localised points of small dimension which escape notice because they are smaller than the hand.

By using the finger tips one may identify small holes in the etheric body, and particularly in analysing the spine.

What the chiropractors say about the spine to be very important, and once again, getting a free flow of energy up and down the spine itself can help symptoms in other parts of the body.

The energy canal of the spine may be no more than an inch wide. With the palm of the hand we miss such a narrow area, but using the fingertips in the same way, one may identify energy blocks, vertebrae that are giving trouble, and particularly at the base of the spine, by following them down the legs, see whether major nerves down like the sciatic or sacroiliac and find whether they are functioning correctly. By boosting the energy through the fingertips and using it as a pointer, or like a laser gun, the free flow of these energies may be re-established and once again the results may be checked.

In conditions of half-light, when I am doing this, I often see what seems like sparks of white light coming from my fingers.

When one has determined that there is a lack of energy in the links producing arthritis, rheumatism, etc, reconnecting the meridians, with the pointing finger is effective. This is a treatment that often needs several repetitions, particularly with old people. I remember in Salamanca, a dear old lady who often came to see me from an outlying village dressed in the traditional widow's black and doubled up with arthritis and rheumatism. She improved gradually, and eventually just came back occasionally to say "Hello", and presents me with a few bottles of wine from her village. Once again, in geriatric medicine, straightforward healing of this kind could be very beneficial, and improve the quality of life.

One points at the base of the neck and run the finger down the arm, (without touching), to the end of each finger. Do it five times. With the legs, from the base of the spine to each toe. When I have done this with an acupuncturist present, they have agreed that the same effect has been achieved as with their needles.

The finger can also be used in this way to stimulate individual organs, but so can holding the palm of the hand next to the organ in question. It is also highly effective in promoting the knitting together of broken bones.

The key to it all, of course, is visualisation by the healer in a high form of consciousness.

Chapter 10

The Nature of Disease

I have alluded in the narrative so far to various conditions which can be alleviated and cured by healing, and if my statements are correct, it does imply that disease is certainly not what conventional wisdom of orthodox medicine suggests. Of course, there is the willing acceptance of trauma as a primary cause of certain conditions, but then how do you identify it without a long dialogue? The healer may say. "There is evidence of trauma. Can you think back to what it might be?" and in nine cases out of ten, the sick person comes up with the answer themselves.

It is now accepted that the majority of diseases are not necessarily caused by accident or infection.

There are enormous pressures on doctors today to alleviate symptoms through drugs and surgery, rather than find the true causes are enormous. How can they have time to find the psychosomatic cause when they have got 30 people waiting in surgery?

It would appear that GP's would benefit enormously from developing these relatively straightforward disciplines and exercises, being able in two minutes flat to see a whole new dimension to the ill-health of their patients.

Most doctors will accept, that of the alleviation of symptoms sometimes becomes more important than the healing of the illness. Medical science is deeply rooted in non-spiritual physics.

It is interesting to observe that emotion washing, as practised by certain sects today, has a profound and persistent effect. The cultivated withdrawal of affection is a primary weapon and, when fear has been established within the new member, new suggestions are programmed in. Those sects I have studied have no crown chakra at work. Some seem happy, some seem automata, but none of them have a crown chakra, which must say something about their spiritual freedom.

The evidence that disease starts in the energy bodies, and therefore in the hologram is, to me overwhelming. I should say that the etheric is only the first.

You can feel the onset of a diseased organ before it manifests, and that is very important. A weak energy field around the liver doesn't mean the liver necessarily has problems at that moment, but that it will have if not stimulated energetically. This is undramatic, not miraculous, but the most responsible type of healing. A healer must never seek only apparently miraculous healings.

There is a presumption in all of this that we start out in life with an "all systems go." That there is a basic "idea" of one's perfection at birth and for various reasons we deviate from it. Of course, we get older and die. That is inevitable, but Goethe made the important point with his concept of the "urpflanze", the original "idea" of the plant, which obliges its material manifestation to conform to it. It is more subtle than the genetic code and it resides in the most attenuated sphere of reality. Each one of us has our own original idea, which does include the seed of dying. A healer can get to grips with the "idea" of a person as well, which is pretty extraordinary stuff.

There is a school of thought which says, "Of course, much disease is karmic, and the healer can do nothing about it." Indeed, some people will run away from the sick person so as not to have their own karma affected. That is irresponsible nonsense, and a form of spiritual narcissism, which, if the law of karma is correct, would, in fact, make them worse off in their karmic debt.

What is the law of karma? It is basically to do with reincarnation, it is very oriental, and in particular Tibetan. It states that an individual soul has to return to the earth a number of times until it attains a level of enlightenment which permits it to travel to other dimensions, and no longer have to return here to what one may call the grossest form of reality.

The Druids accepted it. Early Christianity accepted it. Remember that the people asked of Jesus whether he was Elijah come again. Later it was expunged from Christianity for political reasons, when the church became a State institution.

The Law of Karma does make sense of an otherwise unjust world. We are paying for the sins of past lives in this existence. Do you think that it affects you? I would not change anything in my life as it stands if I were satisfied about previous incarnations, and I've been told quite a lot about them by various seers. It's all so complex that I would prefer to forget what they had said.

Jesus healed the leper, by forgiving him his sins. I've often wondered about that – how a healing can be achieved by forgiving someone their sins, Indeed, how do you forgive a sin, and what is sin?

If I were to look back honestly, on my life and were to try and see where I have sinned, there are a number of things that trouble me. I remember killing a robin with an air gun when I was about ten. I hate myself for doing that, now. I do believe that we must respect all life forms, even if we have to kill, be it fish, or a lettuce, it must be done with reverence and for food. I have not killed a human being but I was trained as an infantry officer in the army.

That is not trivial. I have hurt people I would prefer not to have hurt, but there are times when you can't avoid it, but I never hurt anyone just for the sheer selfish pleasure of doing it. How much better to avoid acts of revenge even when apparently justified.

But how do we account for childhood leukaemia?

Magdalena and I became particularly absorbed in the case of David, a three-year-old in Salamanca, with leukaemia. The initial treatment of simply boosting his fields had an immediate beneficial effect. Then he declined precipitately. Magdalena and I were in Greece and learned this on the telephone. Due to the pressures of the trip, we had not thought of him for a few days. We did a big operation at a distance, holding him clearly in our consciousness. The next day there was a dramatic improvement, although I understand leukaemia can go like that.

Some weeks later, he just declined and died. We were sad. Perhaps we should not have prepared ourselves to be sad, perhaps we should have dissociated, perhaps there are lots of things to learn there. The one good thing that emerged was a firm friendship with his parents.

There was a case of Anna, a four-year-old in Madrid, identified as having metachromatic leuco-dystrophy and having six months to live. All medical faculties of the world were consulted and were all equally clear. She would die within six months. I treated her by general boosting of her fields. Looking back on it, I knew sudden onset, the motor faculties decline rapidly because of a certain enzyme is not produced to protect growing nerve end. This stops growth. Anna was fed by oral tube, her speech had terminated, her body movements were limited and only her eye movements were lively. A physiotherapist treated her muscles regularly.

In the event, she lived three years, and grew, which was surprising. Her mother, Ascension, was an angel and was totally devoted to the girl, 24 hours a day. Anna died of choking on her food, rather than of the disease itself, but of course, the disease did make her susceptible to choking.

There are other cases. Why should these children die of metabolic diseases? Is there any order or sense of life? I feel for the orthodox practitioner faced with such cases, (and I don't say that in any cynical way). God knows, healing failed in both cases, for all its successes.

It seems that for all the detail of orthodox medicine and healing, some people are apparently born to die young. Can we make sense of it? If life is not just one random sick cosmic joke, where do we look for order? Is it in that healing of Jesus, when he said, "Thy sins are forgiven?"

My assumption here is that Jesus was supreme in developed consciousness. Now there are those who will say, "Oh, yes, you had something to do with that book, "Holy Blood, Holy Grail," to which I would reply, "There is nothing in that book that desacralizes Jesus." That's if you read it properly. That he was the legitimate heir to the throne of Israel, was the husband of the Magdalene, and that there was issue, doesn't for me, at any rate, reduce the fact that this man was developed above all others in the ability to bring the Christ into him and demonstrate it, the Christ may be in all humanity.

So, I come back to that healing of the leper. "Thy sins are forgiven." Which sins? The sins in this life or in past lives? Are we born to die young for sins in past lives, or sometimes are we born to die young to teach things to those who try to heal us, or alleviate our suffering? Is it all part of some cosmic instruction, and if it is, why wasn't it made right in the first place? That is the problem, in a moral sense, of man trying to make sense of life.

But we are here as healers, we have been able to show that there are subtle energies, which when applied to individuals, can heal, sometimes remarkably, but is there such a thing a karmic disease? Is it to do with forgiving sins? If it is, is it to be once in two millennia that someone exists on the planet who can do it?

Is there something we can learn without indulging ourselves in excessive spiritual pretensions, that can help in these cases?

Chapter 11

Healing Organs

It has already been stated that in many cases problems within individual organs respond to a general restoration of energy. A further stage of healing is an approach to the organ itself.

In this case, with the hand against the body, or at a distance, the same procedure is established as with giving vital energy, but in addition, a specific visualisation of the organ in perfect health should be made and transmitted to the individual in question. Further stimulation may be achieved with the pointing finger, and a further extension of all this may be achieved through psychic or etheric operations. However, to create a metaphysical model for the intellectual acceptance of reality needs a little time, so I'd like to get to that by talking first about distant healing.

There is, also, the whole phenomenon of the so-called psychic operation, about which more later.

Chapter 12

Distant Healing and Diagnosis

Distance doesn't matter, be it 6 inches or 600 miles, although distance does lose out on the suggestion side of things, and straight forward human contact. As I said early in the book, Maxwell Cade established mutually entrained brain rhythms between healer and sick person at a distance, I have been present in Spain and dowsed the healing energy when it arrived from a group of friends in England.

As far as the healer is concerned, he should carry out exactly the same procedures as if the person was in front of them.

There is a curious aspect to all of this as well. Many healers have the custom before going to bed to spend 15 to 20 minutes at distant healing and many tell that on occasions, people will phone and ask to be put on the list. They have terrible lumbago or whatever. The next morning, they will telephone with their thanks. They feel much better, and the healer realises he has forgotten to put them on the list!

I believe that why it works is because at the moment of the telephone call, the intent to do it is formed, and absolute intent is essential in healing. The idea forms at the moment of intent and is a clear illustration that whereas we should only promise to do our best, we should always do it with total intent, which means never being surprised or excited when an apparently spectacular healing takes place. If we are surprised it means we did not have complete intent at the beginning of the operation.

When Tito came to me in Salamanca, beaming all over his face, to tell me that the latest scan had shown his abdominal cancer had completely disappeared, I simply called him an "old fraud." I don't say that to be clever or witty, but as an illustration that there should never be any surprise. Of course it works. That's why we must never pick at it or anticipate failure.

However, we must never be despondent when failure occurs if we have done our best and in the section on karmic healing, I'll try to explain why.

As I said at the beginning, we are in the subtle worlds of idea and consciousness, that's why healing at a distance can take place. Group healing at a distance is also extremely effective. Each member visualises the sick person and all work together in a common pool of consciousness, as it were, as one being.

You visualise a golden hemisphere of energy uniting the group. Interestingly if you stand outside the group this hemisphere is both palpable and photographable. Then you visualise a column of light coming down and away you go, and when its ready the energy just goes. It's not the group's decision, but the energy's itself. Suddenly, pouf, and it's away.

There is another very important aspect of working at a distance, and that is diagnosis. One day in 1987, I was doing a course with the Forest Row Fountain Group and talking about diagnosis with the hand, when Eric suddenly said. "My grandmother used to call her patients at a distance and have their energy bodies in front of her, give a quick and good diagnosis and treatment. I've no idea how she did it.

I pondered that for a while, and with Jenni Lansdowne, who was there that day, decided to conduct a series of experiments with her at a distance. "Send your etheric body over," I'd ask her on the phone. "I'll see how you are today. Hm, your crown chakra is a bit down, or your base chakra is a bit up. What have you been up to?" She should be honoured amongst women as the first person to donate her etheric body to science, just as Magdalena was the first to donate her upper chakras, about which more later. There ought to be a pantheon for them.

How is it done? At first, I thought it needed co-operation so the etheric body was sent to you, but then, when it seemed to be entirely in the sick person's interest, I tried just calling for it and it worked. I also started to check Magdalena every day when I was in England and she was in Madrid. Sometimes I would phone her up and say, "What's happened? You're very down." And she would tell me why and I'd give her a boost.

What was more, with the etheric body in front of you, you could heal just as if the physical body was there. Again, the trick is visualisation in the higher state.

With Sheila Nevins once at Chalice Well, in Glastonbury, I asked another dowser to check what happened to her if she sent me her etheric body. Her energy body reduced by half, from which I conclude that there is an authentic transfer of energy during the proceedings. It is not just suggestion. Thus, a new dimension of healing opens up.

It was also good to be able to check up on the family and friends, or such people as one was treating at the time. Of course, it's a very intimate thing to do and I believe a certain ethic must prevail. It should not be used to pry into people's private lives without permission.

It also it tells much about the true nature of reality and the spiritual interdependence of humanity. As long as it's practised with the sole motive of the other person's good, then it's alright.

I was once asked to compare the Annual Conference of the Radionics Association, a group who practise healing at a distance with a radionics box. After an opening presentation, I was asked whether one had the right to give healing to people who hadn't asked for it, which is an interesting question. My reply ran as follows:

"Healing is about loving. It's our duty to love our neighbour. We don't have to get permission to love, we should always be at it. And if you only apply love, you can do no wrong. If it's not like that, then there's no sense in the universe."

I think the question was partly prompted by the belief amongst Radionics practitioners that they are dealing with an advanced technology. I have worked with many, including the wizard of oz, as he is known in Madrid. My dear friend Manolo, a retired professor of radiology, and around the instruments of the Radionics practitioner who is functioning correctly, there is the same column of light as on a conventional healer, and the same ley line energy connecting the instrument to the sick person. Radionics is a spiritual science, but some people feel more comfortable healing that way because it is a semi-technology, but as I will seek to show in the section on photography of the subtle energies, without the involvement of higher consciousness of the practitioner, it just doesn't work.

Healing and diagnosis at a distance do work and the calling of the etheric body for treatment and diagnosis opens up a new way to heal.

Chapter 13

Psychic Operations

Here is a subject full of controversy, miracles and fraud and I can only comment on my own experiences with any certainty.

It all started one day in the Monastery of St John of the Cross in Segovia, about several years ago. John Leslie was a Brighton healer I had come to know through the Fountain Experiment in Brighton, and I asked him to make up a team of healers from Britain that I was getting together for the first course in spiritual healing that I organised there. It was always the week of Corpus Christi, a Thursday in June. If the Spanish get a public holiday on a Tuesday or Thursday, then they do not work on Monday or Friday either. It's known as a "Puente," a bridge. A quite delightful habit. Corpus Christi is a day of celebration of love, and for that and the Puente the date was both appropriate and practical.

I did not know much about John's methods, only that he was a pure soul. On the Thursday of the course, he was listed to perform the first demonstration.

Over breakfast he said to me. "My doctor's given me permission to do an operation." I was somewhat taken aback, but affected no surprise. I trusted John completely. "That's nice," I said, and wondered with great interest what was going to occur. I was to be his interpreter in any event.

John stepped forward and explained that he intended to do a psychic operation and asked for volunteers. A Spaniard of about 55 years got up and said that he had a problem. He came up and drew up his trouser leg showing a thrombosis in his calf that was all the colours of the rainbow. "I've been told I must have surgery," he said, "Otherwise it will go gangrenous. I'm fed up with surgeons and doctors."

He accepted the volunteer, and stretched him out on the lecture room desk. Some medical doctors in the audience asked to examine him and permission was willing given.

John then went into a trance and in a deep booming voice said, "Gruss Gott" in German, and switching to an accented English, announced he would guide John in a psychic operation on the leg.

First of all, he said he would raise the etheric body out of the physical, and proceed to go through the complete operation on the leg as if it were a real surgical operation, ordering an invisible team of nurses and assistants, calling for scalpels and sutures, then coloured rays of light. He got quite tetchy with a lax assistant at one stage. He sewed up, put the etheric body back into the physical, said "Auf weidersehen," and the normal John returned.

On the Sunday, the day the course ended, we all asked the Spanish friend to pull his trouser leg for a check. Even to my untutored eye, the lesion was half gone. The medical doctors agreed.

The next year he came to the course again. "Up with your trouser leg," I said, and he obliged. His calf was as white as the driven snow. I just accepted it as something real but beyond my comprehension.

Later on, we were able to learn that the apparently German doctor was Albert Schweitzer, the Alsatian famous for his leper colony and his skills as an organist,

I was privileged to count John as a friend over the years, and I was permitted either as interpreter or observer to stand next to him when he was operating in this fashion. Indeed, I was permitted to feel what was going on, and I can only recount that there was no doubt in my mind, using my hands, that the etheric body was above the physical and that things were going on at the point of operation. The results were more often sensationally right than not.

I continued to take the attitude that I was privileged to watch and participate in something that was real, but outside my knowledge.

John fell ill, and after a long illness of two years, nobly borne, and with the love of thousands of people he had helped in the US, Spain, France and Britain, he died peacefully in August 1987. We all die of something, even healers. John was an unsung saint, but I sing of him.

I don't know when the idea occurred to me, but it was certainly after John fell ill, that there might be some way the rational healer, rather than the trance healer alone, could contribute to this type of healing.

Anyway, one day, with a plant, (they have etheric bodies too, and I will try and comment on this in the section on plant, tree and agricultural healing,) I sought to see if, by visualisation, one could move its etheric body outside of the plant. It seemed to work, and with my involvement with the healing courses in Britain, France and Spain, I was able to include, as an exercise of beginners, the healing of plants, showing people how they could boost their vital energy. A curious parenthesis of all this is that a selected plant, having been "healed" by someone, and we always treated them lovingly, would firstly have its field reduced to normal by me, so that the next could practise. When this had been done once and the plant felt safe, and a third healer came to practise, we were able to observe that without any action by us it seemed to reduce its own fields in anticipation, as if it were willing to participate in the exercise. Obviously, we never left it other than "up" and many plants visibly improved during the half hour or so of the exercise.

What I deduce from this is that plants have consciousness and intelligence, (see Christopher Bird's "The Secret Life Of Plants") and co-operate with honest loving folk. It may be what having "green fingers" is really all about.

The fundamental point is that we did establish, that while loving the plant, you could, using visualisation technique, remove the etheric body. We always put it back of course.

Some pennies drop fast with me and some drop slowly. This one took a long time dropping. Eventually it occurred to me, from my experiences with John, that at least on a rational level we had been able to lift the etheric body out of the physical of both a plant and a human for diagnostic purposes, still looking at it from the outside with our hands. We asked what would happen if we put the hands inside the etheric body, and gradually the hypothesis formed that a "psychic operation" could be performed rationally and consciously.

Now in healing, it's always difficult for a novice to know where to start, and the whole idea filled me with trepidation.

As I shall relate later, given my circumstances as a business man, it always struck me as being more useful to try to teach healing rather than practise it regularly, for once you set up your stall, you are morally committed to those who come and who need several treatments. For various reasons I used to go to Salamanca in Spain every month, where in Tito's tailors' workshop, we had a "clinic". One person I saw in his own home because he was condemned to a wheelchair by muscular dystrophy, was Fernando. Now Fernando was a jolly sceptic. "If you can help me Colin," he would say, "Then good. But I don't understand how it all works or even if it works." We had good laughs together. He had an acute mind.

I called on him regularly treating him in all the ways I have thus described so far. One day in August 1987, I went with Magdalena. There was no doubt that Fernando had benefited from the treatments to some extent, more control over his legs, less fever at night, a calmer attitude towards life – or that's what his wife said.

But he was still in the wheelchair. I said to him, "Look I've been working on a new technique which possibly could help you. But I've never tried it on anyone before. Would you permit me to try it on you?" "Feel at home," he said, "Do your worst – or your best" (as an afterthought.)

So, I had him laid on his bed face down. "Look," I said "You are only the patient. I don't need you bothering me while this is going on. You need anaesthesia. Why don't you just take yourself off to your favourite beach mentally, and lie in the sun?" "OK", he said with a chuckle.

It was an important moment for me and I felt very nervous.

I lifted his etheric body upwards. There was no doubt it was there above him. I could feel above and below it.

Now as I understand it, muscular dystrophy is a metabolic disease caused by the bone marrow's failure to produce certain substances. (Please check my memory is correct, readers.)

Breathing deeply, I started to place my hands within his etheric body, and I really could start to feel the spine and the vertebrae. Placing my fingers within the spinal cord, I felt cold, and felt that this was something I had to put right. Through the established visualisation techniques, I felt that I did it. I ran through the centre of all his bones in that way. I felt goose-flesh as I did it, and the onset of panic. "Oh, God, please help me!" I calmed down and completed the process.

I relaxed. "OK," I said, "Come back off that beach." He did. "I felt your hands inside me, Colin," he said, "it was good."

I saw him a month later. He was stable and happy. As I write, I have no further news.

The second one was easier, and in the clinic in Salamanca it started to be a routine affair. God knows what people thought I was doing, waving my hands above them with my eyes closed. It seemed to work however.

Then we decide to hold an advanced healing course in Spain in order to permit Audrey Copland of the English National Federation of Spiritual Healers to certify those who had followed the June courses in the various monasteries. (I should add, for those who think working in a Spanish monastery must be pretty spartan – a lot of mortified flesh, hair shirts, cold and showers – of the ones we have used, they are in the main, standard of three star hotels, have hot water, some have individual bathrooms in the "cells", give you three square meals a day with wine, have a permanent bar/cafeteria operating, permit you to have a cabaret night up to four in the morning, and are the very opposite of the Sabbatarian gloom and misery one may be disposed to associate with them.)

There is one monastery in Northern Spain which I may not name where we tried to run a course, and the abbot was happy to have us. "But no women," he said. "Why not?" we asked. "The last time we had a course here of a spiritual nature with women present, two of my monks ran off with two of the women." We didn't go there after all.

The popular British view of religion in Spain is, I do assure you, very wide of the mark.

Although some Jesuit friends, (by the way, I'm not Roman Catholic, I do go to Mass when I'm in Spain, where the priest is a friend, and I go to services in Buddhist monasteries), tell me they would gleefully have burnt me at the stake some two or three hundred years ago, they actually come to the courses, as do doctors, theatre sisters, nurses and priests. In fact, Spain is far more liberal in its attitudes than France or Britain. France is still rooted in Cartesian snobbery, wrongly, for Descartes was a more esoteric man than he was given credit for, and Britain, which has had no social revolution or army invading for donkey's years, is very conservative in its attitudes, for all its liberties.

None of that is to criticise, only to observe. But it's a strange fact that the many monasteries and convents around Madrid are booked solid for residential courses, be they healing or Zen Buddhism, and the Spanish religious orders almost overnight have turned themselves into study centres, largely of a spiritual nature. A strange revolution is happening in Spain, it's spiritual, and it's lay, and it's welcomed by the religious orders. Of course, it keeps them in business. The numbers of monks and nuns are falling, but while the rest of the world perceives Spain as rooted in church dogma, quite the reverse is the case since the cork came out of the bottle, with the end of Franco's regime. It's not without significance that Spain may be held to be the base chakra of Europe, with Iona at the crown, well, the base is vigorous and sending the energy up to the crown. It really is quite extraordinary and later I'll explain what's been going on with Spanish radio and TV in respect of healing.

Back to psychic operations. The advanced healing course was held in a convent at Cercedilla in the mountains to the north of Madrid. Turan Rifat came from Brighton as an instructor, along with Audrey.

It was the first time I had shared this experience with other healers and in one session I had the three Sibyls, Gloria, Begona and another lady all sitting together. They could see everything. "A little bit to the right," they said, when I was trying to sort out someone's prostate.

Again, in Cornwall, at an English Fountain Group weekend, closet clairvoyants stepped forward to help, seeing what was going on. It really was quite remarkable. Sometimes when a photograph is taken, there are some very interesting energies visible to the camera. One, taken of me at the Monastery of St Thomas, Avila, shows a column of light descending on me whilst I was healing. If anyone thinks this represents evidence of some tendency in me towards saintliness, I may tell you that my memoirs will reveal an earthy side, not all bad, but my prayer to God remains the traditional one. "Make me good, but not yet." I'll go for it on my deathbed, I think. After all, just in time is a current business philosophy.

There is also one of Juan Bravo, priest supreme of Dom Benito, Badajoz, saying a remarkable Mass, in which he and the congregation chatted each other up. I've yet to see that at Communion in an Anglican church. The energies looked like a myriad of candles covering the altar. He permitted me to stand at that altar and make a eulogy to John Leslie, just afterwards. God knows what God must make of ecumenicalism when this happens anyway without comment. I was also asked to read the gospels. In English Catholic circles, such a thing would be impossible.

I would only add that the weekend at St Thomas, Avila, was marked by an intense cold when polystyrene foam lavatory seats would have sold well. Two days later I was in bed with the flu, but well cared for by Magdalena, who used to be a nurse in Hungary before the KGB pressgang got her, so I enjoyed bad health.

The point of it all was that others could see the so-called psychic operations. Where they saw problems, I felt cold in my fingers. It was working in a quite remarkable way, and once again, although I hate to say it, I'll try to deal with why they see and how they see in the chapter on enhanced perception.

During this period, however, new dimensions of "psychic operations" became apparent.

It wasn't just a question of raising the etheric body. You could take out the etheric equivalent of an individual organ, and if necessary, through visualisation, make it three, four or five times as big. Even a gland, a small thing in itself, could be magnified up to the extent one could feel around it and where its potential problems lay, and apparently put it right and return it.

I repeat it's all done through visualisation. Whether or not a profound knowledge of anatomy is necessary, I've yet to find out. Certainly, I haven't got it, but when an etheric organ is in your hands you can certainly feel areas of cold and emptiness, putting them right seems to be significant.

At all costs one must maintain total concentration and total reverence. A friend who was learning, with his hands gently cutting the etheric body, suddenly diverted his attention and started to speak in excited Spanish, waving his hands about. The person whose etheric body it was, and who was a volunteer complained of being disturbed.

I feel that something highly important resides in this experience, and that learning from John, there may be a route to "psychic" operations which requires no need to go into trance – the rational way. It may be that, in truth, blood and guts apart, that is what the Filipino's do in their "psychic" operations.

I do feel, however, that the expression is not suitable for what I have described and perhaps "etheric operation" is better, but it's still not completely satisfactory.

This experience, though important in itself, was the key to another form of healing which may be even more important.

Chapter 14

Healing through Archetypes

Carl Gustav Jung's work on the nature of being of the collective consciousness had always interested me, particularly in respect of community healing. His concept of Archetype, basic ideas that existed in the collective consciousness from generation to generation, and between groups who knew each other not, perpetuated certain attitudes and behaviour patterns, as in the 100th monkey syndrome, and having studied Goethe at university I was familiar with the notion of the Urpflanze.

Betty Walters was a member of the Fountain Group in Suffolk which had within it a Spiritualist Circle. I gather the "in" word now for "channelling", and her son was the medium. Frequently Jung came through and the group sent me a paper on ley lines and the collective consciousness which confirmed very much the general ideas, of the then incipient Fountain groups.

At the Fountain Conference in Exeter in 1987, I was chatting with Betty and asked her if she would ask Jung some questions at the next session, to which she agreed. There were two:

1) Is there an archetype of a virus or other form of infection in the case of an individual, and can the healer heal through it.

2) Is there an archetype of a virus or infectious organism in world terms, and can healers heal through it? (I was thinking particularly of Aids in this connection.)

Some weeks later Betty kindly sent me a tape of the subsequent conversation, in which Jung essentially said "yes" to both, and indeed, his comments on healing were very much in line with what I have tried to outline here, and specifically that we, as healers, are channels for healing sources on other planes.

I thought about all this for some time and in October, Magdalena and I went to a healing seminar in Hydra at Rob and Audrey Browning's delightful centre where we did a lot of initial work on the new chakras, now sixteen, which I will deal with later.

Now, Magdalena feels a personal responsibility for the stray cats of the world, and when she had a house in Malaga had some 53 on her books. Hydra was perfect for her and soon she was in the fish market buying some few kilos every morning and holding court on the quayside, surrounded by cats. The locals found all this slightly puzzling.

In its eagerness to grab a fish, one of the cats scratched her wrist and by the time she got back to Madrid, it was not only infected where she had been scratched, but there were stinging, suppurating patches all over her body.

"What have I got?" she said. "It could be AIDS, I did have a blood transfusion two years ago."

"Well, as far as I am concerned, you obviously haven't been to an English boarding school. I think that you are going to have to be painted violet, which is what they did to me when I had it. It's impetigo, not serious but jolly uncomfortable, and a bit of a business to get rid of."

She looked at me a bit dubiously. "How do you know? Anyway, if you are such a big deal healer, why don't you treat me? What about doing the archetypal healing you've been talking about recently?"

"Maybe I should," I replied, and so set about calling up the archetype of her infection, for the first time in my life, by visualisation. Suddenly in my hands, which were about a foot apart, I was feeling a living thing, it tremored and was shaped like this.

"Maybe that's it," I thought, and clapped my hands together to destroy it.

The next morning, she was worse.

In fact, she was so worried, I decided to take her off to the dermatologist. "I don't go to doctors," she said, as Magdalena practices natural medicine.

"OK, I just want him to confirm that what you have is impetigo, not anything worse." Reluctantly she came along.

He was a young dermatologist and invited her to strip off. He had a quick look, and saw the scar tissue on her neck. "What's that?" he asked. "A gunshot wound," said Magdalena casually. He turned away, as if nothing had been said. "What?" "A gunshot wound," she repeated. He shook his head in some wonder. (Magdalena was shot when she fled across the frontier to Austria, which is her story to tell.) Recovered from that he sat down and said, "You have impetigo." "Are you sure I don't have AIDS?" she persisted. "Absolutely, I'm now going to give you some prescriptions." She bristled. "Shut up," I said in German, "You don't have to take them." He reeled off a list of a dozen things including various anti-biotics, things to put in the bath water, and heaven knows what.

We left and went back to my room. "You're not much of a healer," she said, "Maybe you did it wrong." I thought for a while. "Supposing you did it with love. Instead of trying to destroy it?" "Maybe you're right," I said.

I summoned the archetypes again. Actually, that's a pretty pretentious phrase, but that's how it is. Once again, that living mass was in my hands, but this time my approach was different. What I said was the following: "Look, you are upsetting this person. You belong to the earth. You don't need to be living on her body. Please, very gently, go back to where you belong, and I'm sure you will be happier there." And so saying, and visualising the while, I wished the chief microbe to gently take his flock back to the earth where they came from, wishing them well.

"OK, lets go to the cafeteria next door to eat," I said. We had been sitting down for some ten minutes, and I glanced at her wrist. "That's funny. It looks less angry," I said. She looked as well, and at other parts of herself, "You are right. They have stopped suppurating. Look they don't sting anymore."

Next day, she said, "I think your friends have gone. The places are dry." Within three days the scabs had dropped off, and within ten there wasn't a mark on her body.

This means we can talk to viruses, and that's important.

Subsequently, with infections, we have used the same technique, even calling at a distance. Magdalena twice phoned me in England to say her children were ill with flu-like symptoms. Doing the same thing, the symptoms disappeared. The archetype appeared in my hands in England. On another occasion, she phoned to say that one of her dogs had a terrible condition that caused haemorrhages in the nasal passages. The vet wanted to put her down. She is alive and well today. So is my mother's dog who had the same condition. (See Chapter on Animal Healing.)

Thus, the contact with Jung seemed to have provided a key piece of information. "Love thy virus and invite him to return whence he came." When at Cercedilia in November and Magdalena's impetigo had departed a week or so before, I explained the theory to the group of advanced healers who were there, because I was interested in using this approach to the AIDS problem.

With the three sibyls watching, I summoned the world archetype of the AIDS virus. Please don't believe this is pretentious, it's done in total humility.

What I found in my hands was a cratered sphere, like the moon, or one of those practise plastic golf balls. The sibyls saw it and confirmed it's form.

"Can we do anything?" I asked. "NO", they said firmly, "You are not to touch it. Leave it alone. That's a cosmic order." I did nothing. I cannot comment on why it should be left alone. I only feel what they were saying was right, and it was confirmed by other clairvoyants on other occasions. I offer no conclusions.

We all agreed that individual AIDS sufferers could be treated in this way. Curiously, one sufferer came to see us a few weeks later, all the way from Australia. How he got past the Dobermanns Magdalena keeps, to protect her isolated house we will never know, but he was a bit special.

He explained that he had healed himself from AIDS by diet, meditation and visualisation. I checked his fields, and they were great. I called up the archetype, it was not there. "Have you had a clinical test?" I asked. "Regularly. But where can they tell you, you've got the AIDS anti-bodies? There is no other test available. I've got measles antibodies as well, but I won't get measles again. There is no clinical test to say that you are free from AIDS." Of course he is right, and that's a pity, because we are missing a huge point. Unless we know that a person who must have AIDS anti-bodies who has had AIDS is AIDS-free, how can we begin to identify what has gone on to render those anti-bodies effective and the person AIDS safe? There seems to be a missing piece to the puzzle here.

Anyway, so far as I was concerned, he was AIDS free.

What, at least for me, emerges from all this is that healing through archetypal forms of viruses and other types of infection can work.

This stimulated us to go further, into the archetype of man himself, or in the Goethian sense, "der urmensch", for want of a better term.

Chapter 15

The Archetype of Man

In 1986 I went to spend a few days in Andalucia with my dear friend Jesus Morientes. Apart from the usual conviviality, we sat talking of serious things on evening, and I spoke of my interest in archetypal forms.

Now I don't know the extent to which this is relevant, but visiting Jesus and Juana in Taen, on the occasion of their wedding, they wished to have all their chakras melded together.

We sat discussing the question of the five forms and Juana, who is a secret clairvoyant, commented on the fact that when Jesus practised high Zen, one saw him as light made up of geometrical forms with a spiral form around it. Does it represent the ideal form of human consciousness?

"Let's summon the ideal form of the etheric body of man," he said. I did, and we got this form.

Jesus Morientes as a geometrical form practising High Zen.

The spiral I take to be a dragon vortex of vital earth energy.

We did not know about the higher chakras then, but we did know from Turan Rifat, from his studies of Carlos Castaneda about the assemblage point. That is to say about three inches to the right of the spine, on the shoulder blade, is a point that unites all the energy bodies of man.

It is like a form of cable which eventually goes to the vertical above the head. You can feel it if you think assemblage point. It governs our perceptions in the subtle sense, it's rather like a ships telegraph, and it's important in healing.

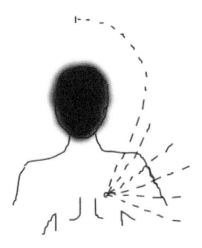

When someone is terribly low the assemblage point can be below the horizontal even, indicating that person's perceptions are very low. The question is posed of the nature of perception and its relationship to health, and whether true health is simply physical.

The interesting thing about the archetypal or ideal form of man is that the assemblage point is exactly on the spine and the cable is vertical. Now, I've had a chance to look at a number of "switched on" people. None of them has demonstrated the vertical. Some have got to 85 degree and one hardly dares talk to them. There is a reason to believe that the vertical cable is something to which humanity may aspire in due time.

Total awareness may be total health, and in that context shuffling off this mortal coil is a minor irrelevancy. We should never be transfixed in the material body, the grossest form of manifestation. What may count for all is that form of self-awareness that regards death as a minor transition. To that extent, however, it remains open to the healer to move the cable from a 30-degree position through visualisation, to a position above the horizontal, and that helps.

Much of disease is suicide. The will to live no longer exists, although one must repeat that the will to live in the physical body is not necessarily the "summum bonum." The will to remove the physical body to pure consciousness is karmically significant. Thus, healing may not necessarily prolong life or consciousness in the physical body, but the extent to which it promotes consciousness in the transition from what we call death in a sentient way to a higher mode of being is an important aspect of the business.

In any event, healers should always check the assemblage point and move it to at least 80 degrees. It stimulates the being, the soul, and it often stimulates self-healing to an import extent.

All this must make rationalist very sceptical, but I repeat, if you get your hands and consciousness going, you can find it yourself. The only limitation to the dowsing faculty is our inability to conceive of what we are able to dowse for. In the next section I will try to explain that whereas we have possibly dealt with an idea etheric form of man, as opposed to an archetype as such, there are geometrical considerations which are significant in the higher considerations of the true nature of health and health transcends the physical body.

Chapter 16

Archetypal Geometrical Forms and
the Primary Essence of Being

Gunther Wachsuth, a contemporary of Rudolph Steiner, wrote a book which is difficult to comprehend at first glance. It is called, "Etheric Formative Forces In Cosmos, Nature And Man." It is not easy to find today, but there is a modern Italian edition. His forms are geometrical. They are obviously and significantly relevant to the empirical experiences I will now try to relate in respect of certain geometrical forms which seem to be crucial to the "being" of the human individual.

We were somewhat confused as to whether what we had experienced in Jaen was the ideal etheric form and not the archetype.

After the experience with Magdalena's impetigo, I can't remember exactly when but during a healing I asked for the archetype of that person (Magdalena) to be given, and a circle, like a ring, that is to say of two-inch thickness and about a foot in diameter, came into my hand. It was perfectly round and complete. On another occasion it was crinkly, and I put it right.

This I put into a perfect circle as well. Experiments with people I believed to be whole in mind, body and spirit showed their circle always to be complete, and completing the circle where it was not seemed to contribute to the healing of the person.

One day, I asked if there were any other forms I should look at and if so, might they be given to me. The double rectangle came up.

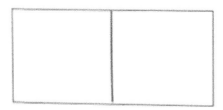

Where all was not well, it would appear thus:

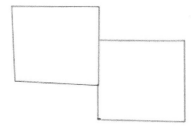

Or this:

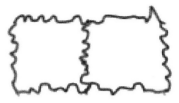

Putting it right seemed appropriate.

Then came another two spheres, like a figure of 8 when they were ideal.

They could be separated or chaotic when they were not functioning correctly.

Then came a flat form, none other than the famous vesical piscis, an esoteric geometrical form, a circle overlapping a circle, and again this could be chaotic or complete.

As a final stage in this form of healing I would ask for all other negativity associated with that person to come into my hands, and where there was some, it would appear as a palpitating mass in my hands. As Turan Rifat had explained the technique to me,

I would visualise the negative energy returning to the "Source" to be converted into positive energy within the general pool. That having been done, I noticed that I was left with a perfect cube in my hands.

It became routine to go through this procedure, and in March 1988, at the Fountain Spring Conference in Majorca, I had a change to demonstrate it to an old friend and healer from Austria, Klaus Brudny. He confirmed the experience, but could not explain it. He recognised its efficacy, and we went to dinner one night to have a chat about it.

I will try and give a resume of that discussion and others, including a session at St Ives, Cornwall, with south western Fountain Groups where the matter was demonstrated and discussed. I should say at the outset that the clairvoyants present do see the forms when they are called out.

Firstly, here is what they are not, we think.

They are not chakras. Except the circle, and I'll comment on this further in Chapter on, "The New Chakras."

They are not to do with the etheric body, or any of the sixteen other energy bodies. They seem to be something more basic even than that.

Are they to do with the gene? Only indirectly, they may be components, in a sense. Someone at St Ives made an interesting suggestion that they represented earth, air, fire, water and either in the Greek way of looking at the essences of reality. I used to feel that this was a naïve and false way of looking at things, but during the last few years, I have had more insight into what they were saying.

In a sense, Mendeleyev, in his subdivisions of the periodic table, was saying something similar, that certain elements are solid, certain liquid, certain gaseous, and others are radioactive. Earth, air, fire, water and of course ether, are the continuum of all things, identified as an essential element of their nature, which was beyond the simple statement as to how many electrons spun around the nucleus. Indeed, if one refers to C W Leadbeater and Annie Bessant's, "Occult Chemistry", when they overviewed atoms and molecules clairvoyantly, they came up with some very interesting geometrical forms. Once again to describe a molecule in the terms of the atoms that go to make it up isn't enough. The form of the molecule is important. Water is not just H2O, but is Y shaped.

The angle of the arms of the Y affects the nature of the water. Of course, the two gaseous airy materials have come together to form a liquid. There are, I submit, "etheric" forces, as Gunther Wachsmuth refers to them, which lie beyond matter as described and expressed by conventional physics.

The St Ives suggestion is intriguing, and for the moment is a good working hypothesis. Which of these five forms are formative in the essence of being? I'm not sure but I'll try and describe my feelings about each.

The circle may be held to be representing the cosmos. In general esoteric lore, this is so, it represents completeness.

The double square rectangle, as I tried to recount in another book, appears to be the form of the Jehovah Elohim in function. Remember it starts as:

The Jehovah Elohim was one of the seven Elohim identified as aspects of God or high spiritual beings by Rudolph Steiner and others, and which hold the programme for the evolution of man's consciousness on the planet earth. It is of the earth. The square is the opposite of the circle in this respect and the double square rectangle may be considered to be the form that represents the Elohimic manifestation in terms of earthly destiny. It's masculine.

The double sphere may be seen as the 8, the number of infinity, and number of the goddess ISIS, see the Tarot of the Goddess. It maybe seen as balance between microcosm and macrocosm. There is an element of femininity and intuition.

The vesica piscis with the circle is a classic feminine form, the vulva, not in the crude sense, but in the sense of a medieval painting in which the Virgin appears in a vision to people inside the vesical. The early Christians used the vesica like this.

People saw it as the fish. I think it had a more esoteric significance. The bringing of the feminine principle in harmony with the masculine again is central to esoteric and spiritual lore.

The cube is a basic building block. The first of the Platonic solids, about which more in the section on the "New Chakras". But I've always been struck by Jesus' statement to the disciplines. "Ye are the salt of the earth." Which also crops up in a very sincere Spanish compliment, "Eres un salado" – you are a salty one. Curiously, the crystalline form of salt is the perfect cube, and once again one asks oneself. "What is the force that makes salt into a perfect cube?" "What makes a snowflake a hexagon?" The more you break natural amorphous forms down to their component parts, the more you see form and number. See chapter on, "Forms of the Genetic Code."

Again, St Peter is always represented as sitting on a perfect cube. Is it saying something about perfection in being?

At the present time, I can neither offer an authoritative explanation of this phenomenon, nor say which is which. But it's there for all to find who so wish. Perhaps we'll understand with more time, but we do seem to be dealing with something that relates in Wachsmuth's terms to formative forces at the quintessential level of man, quintessential meaning "of the five essences", another Hellenic concept. I believe they are a vehicle for very fundamental healing.

One day in February. 1988, I was in Las Palmas, Grand Canary, on business. In the hotel was a health club, to which I went for a sauna. In the sauna area there were acupuncture charts and as I left, the owner, a lovely lady, Nicole, asked me if I enjoyed it.

I asked her about the acupuncture charts, observing that it was possible to arrange the acupuncture meridians without using needles or touching the person, and the talk turned to healing.

I started to check Nicole's fields and those of her assistants and put them right.

I went for another sauna the following day and everybody was bright-eyed.

"We feel so much better," they said, as they did the PR lady of the hotel who had been suffering from depression, and had been summoned for treatment.

"Why don't you give us a course next time you come?" said Nicole. I agreed, and in April, when I had to return on business, Nicole gathered together some 15 people one Saturday, who were interested but knew nothing about the subject.

For me it was an important test. Was it possible to communicate the healing experiences of ten years in eight hours to people who knew nothing?

Briefly it worked.

It was intensive, but the majority were feeling the energies and giving basic vital energy at the end of the day.

That was important for me because I did feel strongly that I had developed, in truth, a rational way to healing, so that people could accept healing as an everyday thing. It should be communicable and comprehensible to everybody who was at least prepared to give it a go, and it shouldn't have to be acquired in the slow, painful, faltering way I acquired it.

So that was useful.

What was also interesting was that there was a suspected AIDS case in the local hospital. The telephonist of the hotel, Nicole and I, went to see him. He was a young homosexual man of about 20, the doctors said he was suffering from an unidentified virus, and was dying. He wouldn't eat, was on an intravenous drip and had trouble with his vision. He was skeletal. I went through the routine check list. I can't remember what was right and what was wrong, but whatever was wrong I put it right. Summoning up the archetype I could clearly feel that spiky, cratered moon effect that I recognised as the Aids virus. Whether it was identical or not I cannot say precisely, but in any event, I invited it gently to go away.

The following morning Nicole told me that the young man's doctors said there was a marked improvement, and he was happy again. A week later Nicole telephoned to say he was eating solid food and putting on weight. I learned later that he eventually died, sadly. I wonder what would have happened had we worked together longer.

I pray the process will continue. Once again it seems that the archetypal way to healing is indicated by Jung works.

As soon as I can I'll do another course in Las Palmas.

I did in December 1989, it was just as good.

Chapter 17

The New Chakras

The concepts that led up to what was called the "Harmonic Convergence" on the 18th August 1987 will not be easy for all to come to terms with, nor is this the place to expatiate at any length upon the general idea. Suffice to say that Jose Arguelles, an American, drew to the attention of the world in general, that there were a number of prophecies of Aztec, Maya, Hopi and other cultural origins, that all had something in common, namely that 18th August 1987 would see the end of an aeon and the birth of a new one, provided enough people in the world came together in meditation to welcome a new impulse which would raise the level of consciousness in humanity.

Elsewhere and a bit earlier in this opus, I have sought to explain that they ley line system as we first observed it, worked on a 7 factor, up to 49 parallels in the lines which are the veins and arteries of the being Gaia, the earth, our collective being.

The 7 factor went to an 8 on Good Friday, 1978, after the grail stone was brought from Andorra to England, and the Glastonbury operation took place. See the book, "Who'd Have Thought It." Eight is the number of spiritual regeneration. Thus, the font and the pulpit are always octagonal, although no cleric I have ever spoken to has been able to explain this.

On August 18th-19th, 1987, the 8 factor went to a 12 overnight, because at the end of the day, so to speak, millions of people around the world came together in consciousness for this event. Spanish National Radio broadcast reminders about taking part for some three weeks before hand.

I was in Glastonbury with Magdalena, and many others that day. Curiously, she felt it more appropriate to be at Chalice Well whilst I was on the Tor. It was totally appropriate. In any event, the Tor put out a massive sun wheel effect, like the spokes of a cartwheel whilst all this was going on. It was then that we found the line system had moved to a 12 factor.

Earlier we had assumed that the 7 factor in the lines of collective being related to the seven chakras of man as he then was.

We assumed now, after the change, that there would be twelve chakras instead of eight. I ought to say that after the shift from seven to eight, the star chakra appeared over the crown chakra. It was a different number of points according to the individual's state of being. It is palpable with the hand.

So, for a few months, we started to look desultorily for the new chakras, not very seriously, because we were not sure about it all.

The Fountain International Annual Conference took place on the weekend 25th – 27th September 1987. The 29th is St Michael's Day, and we hold the conference as near as possible to that. The French Fountain Group decided to hold its Conference on the 26th in a convent in the southern outskirts of Paris, So I went there first and delivered my talk. Here we met Jacques Derlu who is an extraordinary healer and clairvoyant, apart from speaking perfect English. "Ho, ho," he said, "You are right. But tomorrow it with move to a sixteen. There will be 16 parallels to the lines, 16 energy bodies and 16 chakras." Jacques had prophesied certain things in the past and had been right, particularly in the evolution of the Fountain fields.

Anyway, I left on the Saturday night to fly from Paris down to Exeter. We had a jolly conference, at one stage a speaker addressed my mother as "Madame". I said, "That's no Madame, that's my mother," which will give you a flavour of the lack of pomposity and over sobriety of Fountain Groups.

I appraised people of what Jacques has said, and we decided to do the Andorran Meditation for Gaia, (which appears at the back of the book.)

Hamish Miller and Jenni Lansdowne remained outside to observe whether any shift would take place. It did. It went to sixteen.

I don't remember exactly when we first looked seriously at the new chakras, but certainly at Hydra in October, with Rob and Audrey Browning, Connie from Holland, Frances, an American astrologer, Magdalena and myself, some fairly definitive work was done. Things are moving so rapidly now, that one's memory has to race to keep up.

Working together with Rob, Audrey, Connie and Magdalena as volunteers in Rob and Audrey's house, each stretched out and permitted their new chakras to be inspected.

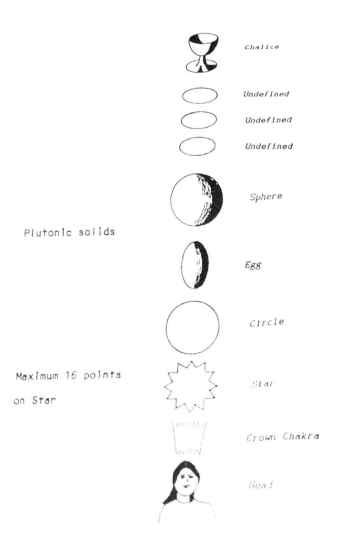

Chalice

Undefined

Undefined

Undefined

Sphere

Plutonic solids

Egg

Circle

Maximum 16 points

on Star

Star

Crown Chakra

Head

New Chakras 1987

102

ᴊb felt very unsteady for a while, but got over it. Others felt OK, even though they were having their parts of their being looked at in the most intimate way.

Rob and Magdalena shared one thing in common. They were both condemned to death by the KGB, but that's another story.

On various occasions apart from this, volunteers have been asked to think of mundane or even naughty things whilst their chakras are being looked at, and they do change according to the mode of the person.

Thus, the star chakra can go down to a blob, or move through 3, 5, 6, up to 16 points. "Get into your star," is now common parlance in Fountain circles.

Then there is the circle. As I've said earlier, it's what comes out when one asks for the individual's archetype. Is this the same thing as a chakra? In this one instance, I believe it is.

The next one is the sphere. What it might mean we can only conjecture. Is it man's connection with Gaia? A lot more work is needed.

What about the egg? Is it the Cosmic Egg, our connection with the cosmos? The curious thing is that it is within the egg that we find the progression of Platonic solids from the cube to the dodecahedron. I can't dowse it in any further detail, but volunteers, and I remember Margaret at Glastonbury, again demonstrate changes in the form of solid according to the way they are thinking.

There are three more blobs of energy, undefined. Some say these are not yet ready to be used. Just as Jacques Derlu says we can only deal with some of the energy bodies at the moment. One

can only feel an energy mass, nothing else, but at the to
is the cup, the chalice, the Grail. At first, I thought it wa.
flower. It was only later I became aware it was a cup, and it's
curious because eggs, Platonic solids, circles and the like are
primordial forms, but his cup is in accord with a human artefact.
It has an octagonal base, in fact it is just like the cup at Wulframs
Eschenbach, near Nuremberg on which the altar rests.

It is open to us to see a parallel form of knowledge, a gnosis,
existing alongside but hidden from conventional wisdom.
Maybe the whole story of the Grail as a cup or chalice, and
illumination, total awareness and cosmic consciousness, is as it
is, because the last chakra of man, his grail, is such a cup.

Alternatively, we see and feel it as the Grail cup because within
our vocabulary of imagery, that the Grail is the supreme
consciousness. Perhaps it's subjective, (none the less real for
that,) and perhaps a Hindu or a Buddhist would feel it to be a
lotus. But for me and for the others, united in the Western
mystical tradition, (see Christine Hartley, "The Western
Mystical Tradition".) It is palpably the Chalice. Anyway, there
it is. Have a go yourselves.

We have to do some more work on this. At least, I believe we
know the ideal forms. As to how one heals through them, the
empirical data base remains to be filled, but having them all
functioning in an ideal form seems to be a new potential form of
consciousness available to man since Harmonic Convergence
and the Exeter Conference 1987.

At a healing seminar in Madrid in January 1990, those present
had a particularly keen interest in new knowledge, and we felt it
right to have another look at the chakras. One of the girls, Rosa,

had developed a particularly sensitive perception, and mine had also become more acute.

A volunteer let us have a look at the upper chakras and Flora, the lady with the perception, tried to see with her inner eye.

Accordingly, we sought to look at the twelfth, and this time I noticed that it had the form of a pair of wings, using my hands, and we generally agreed on this.

The thirteenth was a conical spiral, and fourteenth an apparent sunflower, with petals and the extraordinary internal double helix geometry that the sunflower seeds make.

The fifteenth, variously described as a crystal or jewel by Rosa, seemed to me to have the form of a complex polyhedron, based in triangle, pentagons and octagons.

I think the important thing was that this was carried out in the presence of a like-minded group of people an in my experience such a coming together heightens everybody's general perceptions, so we can hope that these observations were objective. So now the top five of the sixteen are like the below illustration.

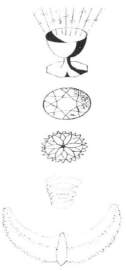

The Top Five New Chakras

During the general discussion, an attempt was made to apply an interpretation on each one.

The angel wings may be determined to represent the archangelic kingdom.

The conical spiral the cosmic vortex or general principle of manifestation.

The sunflower helices the manifestation of Cosmic Light on the material plane.

The polyhedron, or jewel, the first manifestation of light in the spiritual plane.

The Chalice or Grail, pure light or pure divine consciousness.

It is an attempt and absolutely not intended to be "ex cathedra," and I think many people will do much more work on the interpretation.

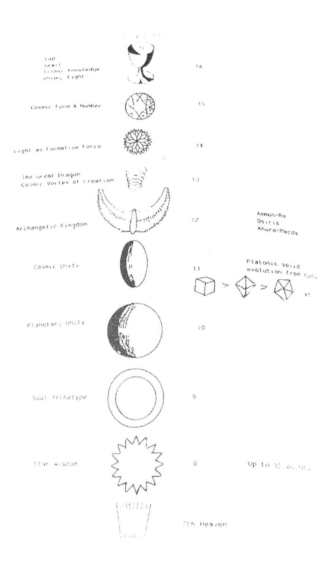

Chapter 18

The Karmic Lattice

During the Majorcan Conference in March 1988, with Klaus, Jenni, my saintly mother, and in preparation for the conference about the figure and person of Jesus, we discussed some of His healings. We examined in particular one statement I mentioned earlier, that the forgiving of sins was the basis of healing. The question arose as to why the forgiving of sins should cause healing, and whether they were sins of this life or past lives. Clearly the removal of guilt feelings would heal psychosomatic disease. In Jesus's case it was leprosy, and thus we wondered as to whether or not He was referring to sins of past lives, leprosy being carried by a micro-organism, and difficult to contract.

My views on reincarnation are ambivalent, but at least it makes some sense of an apparently random world. However, congenital influences and disease certainly do exist.

"I wonder what would happen if I called up someone's karma. Who's to be first" I said to Klaus. Jenni volunteered. Once again, she goes down in the history of this affair.

So, I did, and what I felt to be in front of me was the following form:

32 Steps

"OK," said Klaus, "Do mine." I did, and the same thing came up. Then my mother, the same. Now I do feel that all three of them are whole souls, and the fact that they should exhibit the same characteristics was therefore not surprising.

I accordingly called at a distance the karma of someone I had reason to believe was not so fortunate. It came up with all the steps broken.

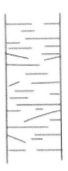

When Magdalena arrived the following day, I checked hers and it was complete.

From time to time, I checked out other people, and sometimes I'd get a more or less broken form, and sometimes this:

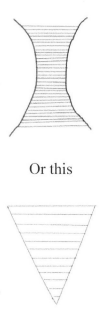

Or this

Which I assume to mean one is dealing with a young soul, if this whole speculation has a basis in truth. This is something that is only two weeks old as far as I am concerned, and I need a larger data base to draw conclusions, but it is a working hypothesis, worthy of further study.

For those of you who are saying, "Who is this man to go around forgiving people's sins?" My answer is, "Just another man." It is open to us all to help through loving our neighbour in any way possible. "It's our duty." Indeed, one should love one's neighbour more than oneself in the Aquarian Age, and if making this lattice whole lifts the burden of karma from someone, I certainly have no right NOT to do it. As long as one acts with love and reverence towards another, then I can see no objection.

Chapter 19

New Aspects of the Karmic Lattice

These two forms of the karmic lattice have become fairly frequently observed. They are:

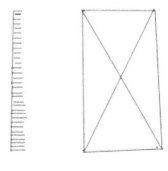

32 steps

We came to call the first the comb, which for those who understand Spanish, produced some hilarity if I did not pronounce the Spanish version correctly. We began to notice that the people who manifested the comb in their karmic archetype shared something in common. They all had vague and general symptoms of malaise, some had received psychiatric treatment, and so on.

Now, I don't remember exactly how the idea occurred, I suspect it was in a conversation with Maria-Asunta, but one of us said.

"I wonder if it is in some way an indication that the soul has not completely incarnated." Which is a potentially curious and novel phenomenon.

I pondered on this concept, and the next time someone came with this effect, I said, "Now I'm going to say something to you which will seem most odd." They nodded in anticipation.

Feeling rather foolish, I said to them, "It seems to me that you have only partially incarnated." The reaction was immediate. "That's right! I've always said I am not properly here." I was relieved, and on other occasions that this has occurred, the reaction has been the same, and on establishing the full karmic archetype, these people seem to develop more confidence, sense of reality and happiness.

The X form however, produced an even more startling proposition. Supposing the X meant the person incarnated on the planet by accident or was suffering karmic complications of an even more profound nature?

Once again, the next time someone came with such an archetype I made a similar approach and said. "It seems that you have incarnated on the planet by accident." The reaction was immediate. "That's right! I've always said I shouldn't be here."

Two young children have recently come with such an archetype. They both have grave physical problems, and in both cases their doctors are unable to diagnose the cause. They are both remarkably intelligent and perceptive. It remains to be seen whether the change of the archetype will help them, it is not possible to discuss it with them, for obvious reasons, but putting it right did have a corrective effect on all the other defective archetypes – kidneys, bones, blood, metabolism, etc.

The implications raised by this hypothesis are very profound. It remains to be seen whether they are factors involved in healing. It seems they may be.

Now it will have been noticed that the ideal karmic ladder is 32 rungs. It was not long before cabbalists emerged saying – "Of course, there are 32 pathways on the Tree of Life."

After reflection, they are of course right to make this connection. If the karmic ladder represents the age of the soul, it follows that a mature soul should have experienced or comprehended all those spiritual experiences that one or many lives offer.

Someone said the other day. "What is the Cabbala?" Now I am by no means versed in the Cabbala, and I parroted what others have said. The answer went something like this.

The Cabbala is a primordial science of relationships between form and number. It may be used to define and analyse all aspects of reality, be they material or spiritual. In the sense that it was first drawn to European attention by Jewish experts in the 15th century from academic centres such as Montpelier, France, and Gerona, Spain, it is not an artefact of Jewish culture. It does involve the Hebrew alphabet, but, to the extent that the alphabet is a primordial and sacred alphabet, it is more correct to say that Jewish esoteric thought has been Cabbalised, and not the reverse.

It may be helpful here to quote from a recent statement by Stan Tenen, Director of Research, MERV Foundation. "We have found that the letters of the Hebrew alphabet, because of the unique means of their generation, represent fundamental directions in a hyperdimensional space. That makes them ideal as elements of a natural algebra for theoretical physics…"

"One result… Has been our development of a compact logical matrix that assigns explicit meaning to each letter of the Hebrew, Greek and Arabic alphabets, and this may represent the rediscovery of the natural language alluded to in the story of the Tower of Babel…

We believe that such an alphabet based on the geometric metaphor we have identified, can specify physical and psychological states simultaneously…"

In these concepts lies a definition of Cabbala, and also an explanation of the archetypes as we find them, and also the 7,000 geometrical forms of the Andorra Stone. (See the book "Who'd Have Thought It," by Colin Bloy and Suzanne Thomas.) In short, it is ELOHIMIC.

In the channelled Hassim tapes, the statement was clearly made that whereas healing karma was now legitimate, it was not just a question of completing the archetype there had to be an understanding by the person concerned.

There is a healer in Spain who will dowse the Tree of Life with a pendulum to identify those experiences necessary to complete an individual's karma, but when they are, as often happens, 100 people waiting for healing, you can't spend too much time on it.

I think that it is fair to say that someone who has completed his karma is someone who practises the principle of pure love in thought, word and deed in respect of all aspects of reality. So, we evolved a short cut to this. Where someone manifests incomplete karma, we try to explain the implications and that it means what was stated in the previous sentence, and ask the person to make a solemn promise to observe that principle for the rest of their lives.

Hassim further said that the mutation of consciousness was in full swing and many people would feel uncomfortable. And if they did not complete their karma in this life, then they would not reincarnate on this planet – some might find this a blessed relief.

Given this new covenant that one should love one's neighbour more than oneself, one is therefore responsible voluntarily for other people's karma, or at least obliged to help where one can. This is the reason why healers are involved with karma.

The implication of Hassim's comments and those from many other channelled sources is that the earth is no longer to be a kind of reformatory for wayward souls, but based on a humanity that is complete in its karma. That is all part of planetary healing, and it may be that the human race has an unsuspected and more worthwhile destiny.

Chapter 20

Healing – The Double Helix

Since Messrs Crick and Watson gained the Nobel Peace Prize for their work in a Cambridge garage in identifying the double helix form of the genetic code, which contains 64 chromosomes, a number of people have made the analogy with the Greek caduceus of the great healer Aesculapius. Magdalena and I visited the ruins of one of his centres in Greece, near Hydra, in October 1987. The caduceus has two intertwined serpents around the staff and is a symbol outside pharmacists in many countries.

During 1987, it occurred to me that it might be possible to call out the etheric form of the genetic code from people. So, on the occasion of an etheric operation I did. The following form appeared:

In cases of metabolic disease such as muscular dystrophy and neuro-motor conditions, it did appear that certain of the knobs, which I take to be chromosomes, were missing, and according I put them back. I feel that this all sounds pretty pretentious stuff, but I do think that I should retell this story exactly as it happened. And if this is a dimension of healing that will help others to do the same, well, I'm pleased.

It may all sound a bit Promethean but I do feel in the Age of Aquarius man's exploration of the etheric and other worlds will be dramatic, and permissible.

In the cases where the missing knobs were put back, there is evidence of improvement. Only time will tell, but once again I want to offer this to other healers as a potentially valid line of enquiry. Of, course, we are dealing with a different metaphysical model from the conventional, that is to say that man's reality is not circumscribed uniquely by his physical body. There are many energy bodies as well that go to make up the whole and that's what I'd like to get on with next.

Chapter 21

What's Behind DNA?

When Clive Wood made the comment, about DNA repairing itself, it set of a chain of thought in my head, which only came to rest some months later. I was staying with Maria-Asunta in Barcelona in November 1991, and the matter had come up again in conversation. "Can't make it out," I said

Denise had also phoned to say that Nick, who had had one healing two weeks before for leukaemia, had just been told that he had degenerated rapidly and had a week to live. Previously it had been six months.

I had another look at him at a distance, and all that had been done with the energy bodies, the archetype, the DNA, etc, was still in place. "I can't make it out," I said, "There has been no reversion at the etheric level, but I'll continue to work."

As I did, the question of what was behind DNA surfaced again in my mind. And for the first time, I asked for the archetypal form of what might be there, if there was such a thing. This is what I got.

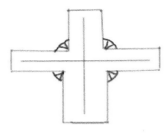

An equal armed cross, and inside it in each arm sixteen small circles, (inner cross).

The first comment was that in some ways it was what one might call a different array of the 64 genes in the DNA, not in the intertwining spirals, but in the form of the equal armed cross, and with a larger circle around the centre as illustrated.

Of course, the equal armed or Greek cross was the first cross used by the Templars, and if the theory was right, it was also the first manifestation in the form of dragon energy, as seen in the first Fountain Experiment – see the book "Who'd Have Thought It" by Colon Bloy and Suzanne Thomas

The Greek cross is the basis of the chequer board when you work it out thus:

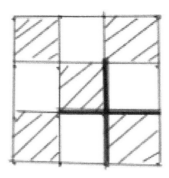

It seems to represent the basis of the first energy body of both the human and the world.

The miniature chequerboard is what the dowser will find around a living organism, human, animal, plant after received vital energy, and for that reason at the beginning of this chapter, I made the remark that the equal armed cross is the first manifestation of the dragon energy, which manifests to dowsers as spirals and is one of the two ley energies in spiritual healing.

That same day as I was given the apparent form behind DNA, I was reading an article by H P Blavatsky in which she spoke of the breath of Cybele the many breasted goddess of the Greek pantheon, and daughter of Coeius (heaven) and Terra (Earth.)

"Indeed, the genealogy and the myths attached to it show Cybele as the personification type of the vital essence whose source was located by the ancients between the Earth and starry sky, and who was regarded as the very "fons vitae" of all that lives and breathes."

"Fons vitae" means "Fountain of Life."

To me this seemed a powerful metaphor pf the energy used in healing when the column of light descends upon the healer from the heavens, and the spiral dragon energy of the earth is drawn up as well, the two combining to permit the healer to pass vital energy to the sick person.

Thus, the equal armed cross would seem to be the geometrical form that such a subtle energy field takes, and that the motive force behind the DNA should be that plus 64 circles, or etheric genes in the form of a cross certainly had a basic logic with this operating context.

I then asked, as my daughter Tammy would. "Is there anything behind what's behind the DNA?" and to my surprise, this was given.

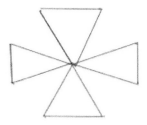

Having taken note of that, I then asked, "What's behind what's behind the thing that's behind the DNA?" To that I get no answer, others may, I may one day, there may be no answer, or perhaps the time has not come, be that as it may. Should it be the cross of the eight beatitudes?

It occurred to me that the difference between the traditional form of the DNA, which is two serpents entwinning, (or dragons – it's the same thing,) and the cross form may reside in Cybele's breath.

Terra, the dragon, is one thing – the light of Coeius, heaven, is another. When they combine the "fons vitae" is established.

Thus, a more effective form of the DNA, more structured, more compelling, is established on the equal armed cross. We had long suspected the Templars knew a thing or four.

Well I thought, let's have a look at Nick's DNA at this level, and thus it was:

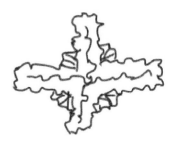

Basically, a scribble, but the circle of his archetype form was very strong. He certainly was a strong honest person who had discussed his illness with me in total frankness. "I've got three months to live," he had said with a smile, and had been entirely open.

I had at the first session noticed that his DNA was defective in the established leukaemia mode and also that there was no energy on the lower part of the spine, and I had got the etheric form of the DNA right, and the workings of the lower spine, where I had always felt the main production of the red corpuscles to be, which is why I told Denise it was still alright by me.

Maybe I had been given some new knowledge at the right time, and I was able to restore the defective pre-etheric DNA to what I considered to be the given correct form, as shown earlier. When I say "I", the reader will know what I mean, at least, it was my visualisation.

The following evening, I received a phone call from Nick, as I picked up the phone, I geared myself to make a maximum effort to raise his morale, and reached for Maria-Asunta's hand in moral support.

"Hello Colin. Have you been up to something funny with me?" he said.

My heart sank further, but I clung to the impression that his voice was cheerful.

"We've all been working for you in the group here.".

I waited for what he was going to say next. That all thoughts

"Well. I can only tell you that when I had my blood test this morning the doctors couldn't believe it. My white corpuscle count has fallen from 150 to 6. (I didn't know what that meant in that instant). It's wonderful news, but the doctors are astonished."

I thanked him for having the kindness to phone me from England, and taking hold of myself, said that the most important thing he could do now was to stop being astonished himself, and calmly accept what the doctors had said as a logical consequence of what healing had done, it was only to be expected. It was over, it was to the future that all thoughts should now be directed.

I gave Maria-Asunta a homily on self-doubt in healing, she gave me the Spanish equivalent of two fingers, wrote this chapter and went to bed.

But before I slept, I gave thanks that we might have been given yet another piece of vital information. I suspect that somewhere in the Chaos Theory of mathematics, things will become clearer with time and study. Perhaps the Strange Attractors are our visualisations and those of God and His legion.

To be added to a list of quotes of reviewers of future editions. *This book is either a cleverly-constructed fantasy or desperately important for the future.*

Over the next few months Nick had ups and downs, but his blood count steadily improved. His wife phoned to say that the pathologists were amazed.

The only factor that wasn't improving was the platelet count, but his morale was good, and we set to work in Barcelona to see how best we could help.

I asked for the archetype of the blood, and asked for the sections in which the three factors occurred, and was given numbers four and five thus:

I then asked for the three factors of the red and white corpuscles plus the platelets.

Red

White

In Nick's case the red count, (after two or three weeks healing, by many people,) was up to ten, and the white count around three, but went on increasing daily to about ten.

The platelets came out as ten sixteen-point stars.

Nick was at three, and there was a perceptible improvement to five in the next couple of weeks, taking us to Christmas, which I spent in Brighton.

The day after Boxing Day there was a message on the answerphone to say that he had died at 7pm that day. My heart sank, and all the self-doubt returned, together with obvious sadness.

Two days later the phone rang, and it was Nick's wife.

"Look." She said. "I'm phoning you to say thank you for all you did for Nick. You gave him strength and happiness. He survived much longer than anyone dared hope for. He had a happy Christmas, as he had wished, and died quietly in my arms with total peace of mind and total dignity."

I scarcely knew how to reply. It appeared the final cause was a brain haemorrhage, the platelets not having increased enough. I thanked her for her kindness in having phoned, and sat down to think about it all, first taking the trouble to make sure Nick has passed over completely, which he had.

Of course, as I had always been taught by John Leslie, making death peaceful and a good passing is a very great healing. I hasten to say many healers were helping Nick, not just me, and I took comfort on reflection that it had been a privilege to know such a courageous and honest man, and yes, it was fair to say that in his case spiritual healing had helped him at the most critical time. For that I gave thanks to "them upstairs."

I further feel that the new understanding about the cross behind the DNA has proved significant and would become increasingly so in the future.

Chapter 22

The Energy Bodies Of Man and Visitors

Whereas we seem to have got some sort of handle on the first four energy bodies, the rest remain a great mystery, for the lack of concepts with which to test them. Recently, however, I feel we have got something to put forward, at least in terms of their dowsable forms up to 14.

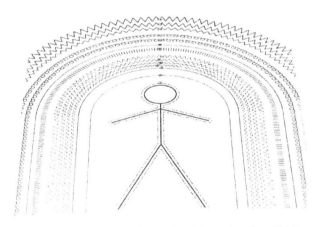

All help and suggestions as to understanding welcome.

We have dealt with the etheric body in earlier sections, the first energy body around man. Jacques Derlu, French healer explained in lecture that there were 12 ley line factors, and on the next day there would be 16. These represent the basic factor of the ley lines that go to make up the collective being of humanity and its habitat, GAIA, our planet. He also said that it was unlikely in our lifetimes that we would understand much more than the first 6.

In a sense, he is talking about Carlos Casteneda's cosmic egg, in which man lives, similar to the way that Jesus Morientes lectured to the Fountain Conference in 1985 at Brighton.

It's rather like this:

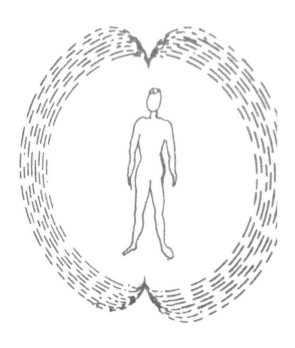

I can feel them all but understanding them is a different matter. That there should be a relationship between the number of man's energy bodies and the predominant factor in the ley lines is perfectly logical.

The only concrete experience I can offer about the additional energy bodies after the etheric is the following.

One day in October 1987, I received a phone call from the mother of Debbie. She explained that Debbie had been committed to a psychiatric clinic because she had been hearing voices, not very agreeable ones, which excited her to violence and suicide. She was diagnosed as a schizophrenic.

I immediately asked her parent to come around with photographs. I had met Debbie on a previous occasion in relation to a lodger in her house who found a ring in the street which had presented problems. Apparently, these had cleared up.

As by that time the business of calling people to one had developed, I asked Pat, her mum, to visualise her for me, and there she was in front of me. Her basic etheric body was virtually non-existent. I put that right and called up the second energy body. I saw that she was a natural psychic.

Just above the right shoulder was a pulsing mass. It was difficult to identify precisely what it was. I can only describe it as an unwelcome friend, perhaps what the Cabbalists call a larva, an elemental in other terms, a form of being which attaches itself to weak or sensitive people in a vampiric way. A low-level form of being which in a sense is like a psychic tapeworm and which feels like a parasite at the subtle level on its chosen host, drawing energy from them.

This is purely theoretical, although there is much in the foregoing that is the fruit of empirical observation, but I am a little lost in this section, and must depend on supposition.

Taking this palpitating mass in my hands, I sent it gently and lovingly back to the "Source", to be converted into positive energy. Well, what more can you do?

Magdalena and I went off to Hydra the following day and on my return, Pat phoned me to say that Debbie was better. I asked if I could go to the psychiatric hospital to see her and it was arranged. Her energies were still low, so I put them right, but we had a good dialogue and there was no evidence of her "incubus".

The affair progressed well, and she was allowed out of the hospital and came to see me again, each time visibly better and more understanding of her being. The negative voices had disappeared.

I reasoned with her about her psychism and asked her if she would prefer for the moment if I cut off her psychic sources. She said, "Yes." "When you want them back, we can open them up again." This refers to the throat chakra particularly, and the assemblage point.

Since then she has progressed well, is putting on weight, wants to get a job and shows every sign of "normality." Later when, like Rudolph Steiner, she wants to revert to psychic and intuitive perceptions, but under the control of her rational mind, I think I can help her sort it out.

The success of that operation was brought to another person, a Polish lady living in Brighton and treated by the same doctors, and she asked to see me. She was very sweet and gentle lady, and on looking at her it was evident she was a similar case. She had been on medication for some years as a schizophrenic. I went through the same procedure, for she had a similar "visitor" to Debbie's. Two weeks later she phoned me to say that she was healed and happy.

So far this is the limit of my experience with other energy bodies. There was the case of Charlotte, who was very similar, but I'm not sure what else there is to look for at this level. Jacques says that healers today can only deal with the first six energy bodies in any event, so hopefully, what I am recording here are signposts for future healers who come after. Maybe I'll know more in another 10 years, but that's the state of the art as far as I'm concerned at the moment.

On the other hand, since Harmonic Convergence, things have moved in a quantum sense, so perhaps more will be revealed.

However, 16 energy bodies are there, and you can feel them.

Chapter 23

Healing by Radio

Whereas I travel in many counties, it is in Spain where I found the most willing acceptance of all this, which is, at first sight, curious.

The conventional view of Spain is of a country rigidly locked into the most abstruse dogma of Roman Catholicism. It is true that General Franco had a pretty clear, agreement with the Vatican, which effectively reaffirmed Roman Catholicism as the established religion of the State, and gave it very definite privileges.

I was in Spain when Franco died. It was a moving occasion. For although the word "dictator" is emotive in the general ethos of western democracy, Franco did hold Spain together, keep it out of World War II, and created before his death the mechanism for the return of Spain to a constitutional monarchy and a parliamentary democracy. There is no precedent in history for a dictator to do that. Personally, I believe that he did command a majority of support of the Spanish nation and that's why it's moving to observe his obsequies at very close quarters.

Thus, to a certain extent, the idea of a rigid, established Roman Catholic Spain under Franco is not quite correct. After the horrors of the Civil War, which left full responsibility to Franco during his lifetime, there was a general acquiescence that they would return to the general thrust of Western European ethos.

This was not inhibiting to intellectual or cultural development, albeit not publicly demonstrating. Granted the Picassos and Casals had been obliged to live in exile, but it would be wrong to assume that Franco's Spain was somehow like Hitler's Germany where a fundamental attempt was made to change the cultural, intellectual and spiritual ethos of the nation out of the heretofore accepted Western Judaic-Christian tradition.

There was an argument amongst Spaniards to knuckle under and accept the restrictions and disciplines in order not to experience once again the horrors of the Civil War.

May I state quickly that I was an active member of the British Liberal Party, voted Liberal, and regard Liberalism as the only intellectually respectable political philosophy available, but I do feel that Franco's Spain was a very difficult situation, particularly as the Spaniard is ebullient and excitable. History may well accord Franco the unique status of dictator who did not seek "Apres moi le deluge," or his own dynasty, but simply to return his nation to the "status quo," and it is a marvel to behold the scenes in the Spanish parliament when Juan Carlos was proclaimed King after his death, and the emotion of his funeral.

Spain today, is a full-bodied member of the Western Liberal democracies. Without Franco, it would never have happened.

Anyone who feels that Franco was a fascist had better re-read history. He was a Spaniard steeped in its traditions. Authoritarian he certainly was, and, in a large sense, that is why against all apparent odds, spiritual healing is now a matter of public comment in Spain both on radio and TV, and it will be a great surprise to learn that in October and November 1987, Magdalena and myself and a Roman Catholic priest took part in a programme about spiritual healing on Spanish National Radio.

The cork came out of the bottle at Franco's death, one is obliged to comment that the Spanish released the pent-up emotions and desire to enquire in all directions, be it pornography or a new search for spiritual reality.

Today in 1988, it is impossible amongst the many monasteries and convents around Madrid, to book a weekend's course unless you give a minimum of nine months' notice.

Something very important is happening there. Now they are well endowed with institutions, but they welcome any form of spiritual group, be they Buddhists or healers. I cannot say the same for Britain. France, yes. Austria, yes. But suddenly that apparent bastion of Roman Catholic faith, apparently transfixed by Vatican dogma, is now the most liberal of all.

Every course that we have given, be it at the monastery of St John of the Cross at Toledo, or Segovia, or Majorca, or the Monastery of the Valley of the Fallen, where Franco is buried, we have always welcomed Roman Catholic priests, whom we now call our own. That sounds impertinent, it isn't intended to be.

They say the Mass to the Anglicans, Roman Catholics and non-aligned alike. They are extraordinary masses. They talk to the groups during the Mass and invite their participation in dialogue. We laugh together during the Mass, and sing. I, as an Anglican and having recorded the fact, have nevertheless been invited to read the gospel, take communion and deliver homilies about healing, and in particular about John Leslie. I'm only an Anglian by culture, and when asked what my church was, I say where there is a good priest and a good congregation.

Granted, it is all under a Christian canopy, but the basic humanity of it is something I have yet to experience in England. Certain Anglican priests have become all snotty and said that healing should only take place within the Anglican church.

There is a photo of the Reverend Juan Bravo saying Mass to our healing group. It shows the same energies, as during psychic or etheric operations. That's the trick we all have in common.

My first friend in the Roman Catholic church in Spain was one Jose-Maria, Jesuit priest and dowser extraordinary. We spent much time together, thanks to the introduction made by Enrique de la Clerva, my dear business associate in Madrid, his uncle Juan de la Clerva, invented the autogiro, precursor of the helicopter and was killed in an air accident at Croydon airport. You may remember that Jose-Maria said he would have had me burned at the stake three hundred years ago. My retort to him was that one day he might become a decent Christian, and told him the story of the meeting of the Roman religious orders, When they fell to quarrelling amongst themselves as to which was the most favoured by God. As they were approaching violence, their heads asked the Archangel Gabriel to go to God and asked for a ruling. When he returned, he had a letter which said:

"All orders are equal in my sight.

Signed

God, S J"

He laughed, and we have been firm friends ever since and in some pretty remarkable circumstances.

All that having been said, it is perhaps strange to record that I have been permitted over 24 hours of prime radio and TV time on various Spanish National radio stations to speak of these matters in the last five years. But the most important programmes of all were those when healing was actually going over the air waves.

In 1987, I began a series of radio broadcasts on a programme called "Espacio en Bianco," presented by Miguel Blanco, with whom I became firm friends. He had been introduced by a mutual friend and scientific journalist who also took part in the programme, Enrique de Vicente.

I did a few talks on the Knights Templar, the book, "Holy Blood, Holy Grail," and a talk for an hour about healing. As we sat in the studio after it was over, Miguel said. "That was good, there's a lot of interest."

I thought for a moment.

"Why don't we do healing over the air waves?"

"What do you mean?" he said.

"I mean instruct people how to heal and send healing energy from the studio."

His eyes lit up. "Right on!" he said, or the Spanish equivalent.

It was about this time that Magdalena and I met. She had needed a healing for all sorts of good reasons, and we knew each other immediately on sight.

"Look. We must work on this together. Apart from that it's very important that the feminine voice alternates with the masculine. But I don't know where to begin," I said.

We began to think how it should be done. At this point I had the pleasure of attending a wedding in England of Richard, son of Michael Bentine. Doris Collins and Betty Shine were there, two well-known healer clairvoyants, I told them of the project and sought their sound advice.

They were both clear that the audience should participate in the healing of those around them who were ill or in need of help, that other healers should concentrate on the studio, and that music of the right sort should be used. Thus, it started to take shape.

We began to write a script which involved putting people into a relaxed state, explaining about the third state of attention, how to plug in and visualise, placing their hands on those near them and how the people in need of healing should participate. Then we would have two minutes of music only and go on to distant healing, encouraging people to send healing in the same state of mind to those they knew needed healing but were away, even in another country, just as I described distant healing earlier. Again, two minutes of music and then a gentle return to normal consciousness.

Our voices were to alternate. Magdalena's voice is particularly suited to this type of work, and she speaks virtually perfect Spanish in spite of being Hungarian.

"Do you know," I said one day preparing the programme, "It's a great impertinence that a Hungarian and an Englishman should be sending healing to the Spanish people." But there it was.

We asked the sound engineers to use the Largo from Dvorak's "New World Symphony" as background music.

Then all of a sudden, there we were at twelve to midnight, in the studio during July, 1987. We both felt odd. There had been no rehearsal and no publicity, but we had a keen desire to accomplish well what was probably the first ever public healing broadcast. Healers in the UK, France and Spain all joined in.

The introductory music started to roll. Miquel began to explain what was going to happen. He asked us questions and at 12.30am we started the meditation and proceeded as outlined for the next 15 minutes.

The sound engineers really got the music right, getting the crescendos of the "New World," at the end of each two minute period of healing.

It was over. Everybody seemed happy. Magdalena and I went home somewhat drained.

A few days later, mail came in, encouraging but not enormous. The audience seemed pleased, but audience research showed that the night had not been well subscribed to. There had been a late night film on TV, and no audience publicity.

Later that week, Miguel said, "It was a great success in the circumstances, and the station director was pleased but said we should repeat it, do it better, and he would allocate two hours to the programme instead of one, give advance publicity and get us 30 minutes on the television the same evening before the programme. WOW!

What Miguel wanted was a direct link to other healing groups throughout the world and make it a genuine International event. We sent out a circular to Fountain Groups around the world. We also wanted to tackle people who had received healing.

At the advanced healing course in Cercedilla in October, Father Juan Bravo, priest of Dom Benito near Badajoz, attended. He had been at the course in the Valle de los Caldos in June. He and Magdalena took to each other. Remembering the impertinence of two foreigners healing in Spain, we asked him to help us and participate. He was somewhat taken aback. "I'll get unfrocked!" he said, but was smiling. We gripped him between us, and he put up no further resistance. Miguel like the idea of having a Spaniard and a priest taking part as well.

And so it was, Magdalena, Juan and I formed a firm spiritual bond and he had a good laugh when we told him he was to participate in a healing broadcast in Spain as a priest, with a former KGB agent, and a former member of British counter-intelligence. The sheer incongruity of the whole affair was remarkable.

I telephoned Sheila Nevins in Cornwall, and told her what was afoot. She didn't mess about. With 48 hours some 1,600 notices were winging their way around the world and within a week feedback came in and we had a long list of groups ready to participate in many countries.

I phoned Enrique de Vicente. "Things are a bit slow here, but we are putting out publicity on the programme," he said.

I told him what Sheila had done.

"We'd better wake up," was his reply.

I flew back to Spain the Wednesday before. I had roughly worked on an expanded script for the meditation. Magdalena took it over and spent Thursday night typing it out in better Spanish than mine until 4am.

Soon came the day in November. At 7.30pm we went to the RTVE studios and found to our surprise, we were to follow the main news at 7.30 on Channel Two using the slot for news comment, and they had given permission to overrun by 10 minutes because of interest, giving us half an hour to discuss the radio healing programme to go out on Radio Cadena Nacional at Midnight. It was a bit overpowering.

In the event, the interviewer was not that well briefed. I put my best suit on and demonstrated how to feel his fields. Juan did his thing as a priest, pointing out that part of the Christian ministry was healing. Miguel gave details of the programme to come. Magdalena smiled from the side lines. Then to the studio, and there began what I can only describe as one of the most remarkable events of my life.

After a brief introduction we got down to business, and Miguel and Enrique started to call up Spanish healing groups, who gave their support and testimony.

Suddenly we had a girl on the line who had been healed of a large growth in the neck by Juan. Miguel examined her very closely and critically, and was satisfied an authentic healing had taken place.

Then we had Roger Brown of the Adelaide Fountain Group on the line from Australia. He gave his support and testimony, we exchanged greetings. I was very moved, and things started to flow at an exhilarating pace.

Then came Dina Dewash from Belgium, (in French), Klaus Brudny from Vienna, (Magdalena talked to him in German), Fritz and Bart from Holland, (in English,) all enthusiastic and sending greetings.

"A right Tower of Babel tonight," commented Miguel happily.

Then a young man from Salamanca who had been confined to a wheelchair gave his testimony quite unequivocally. "A few days after Colin had placed his hands on me, I started to get strange sensations in the lower part of the body, and realised that I could walk."

You cannot believe the wave of emotion I felt and the tears that came.

Then came Manolo from Madrid who has a form of bone disease, and could only sleep with the help of drugs. He said he didn't need them anymore and the pain had gone.

Then another person, treated by Juan, and so it went on.

All to quickly it was the one o'clock news. We sat back for a while bemused then off we went again. Then Miguel said he had my mother on the phone. So, there I was chatting with my mother in London over the radio. All her group were participating.

Next Miguel phoned the group in Salamanca where I had been going regularly and spoke with Carmen and Domi, the organisers. They commented on various healings that had taken place there, and there were two more with them who gave their testimony. Suddenly Miguel winked at me. "Now I have a wicked question to ask. Does Colin charge you?" Dear Carmen got quite excited and said "No," in indignation. Miguel smiled. Later he said it was very important to establish that, as the station would never have given so much air time to someone who practised anything professionally.

Then came Sheila from the Fountain office in Cornwall. "How many people are there with us tonight?" Miguel asked. "That's a bit difficult to say," she said slowly. I wondered what was coming next. "Here in Cornwall we have 22 different groups participating, and individuals who are actually listening in to your programme. In Devon there are 17 groups, but I couldn't tell you how many people there are." We exchanged greetings.

We had planned to phone Michael Bentine and Fountain friends in California, the Medicine Man of the Cherokee Nation in New York, the Fountain group in Switzerland, in Munich, in London, others in Spain, but time had run out. In the studio were the Trappmans from England, who photographed it all, Rafael, the President of the Madrid healers, a medical doctor, the Station Director, the interpreter, you could hardly move!

The format at the healing section of the broadcast was the same with improvements but we used the occasion for another first, community healing or Fountain "work", getting the listeners in each town and village in Spain to go through the visualisations that improve the level of consciousness in their areas, making things go better, reducing violence, accidents, etc., (which is the subject of another book "Who'd Have Thought It," by Colin Bloy and Suzanne Thomas.) For that, I insisted that the only possible music was the second movement of Rodriguez Aranjuez Guitar Concerto, which always sends quivers up my spine.

And so, we were to do it again. Juan and I alternating with Magdalena. The column of energy on the table was intense. There must have been up to a 1,000 or more healers beaming in on that studio from all over the world. It was unbelievable. Strangely enough, healing energy can be carried on the air waves. I have heard some of Uri Geller's broadcasts when listeners have found watches and clocks starting again when he has concentrated. I remember on the Jimmy Young show with Uri Geller when a policeman in Bromley phoned up rather bitterly to say he was just going on duty and putting his helmet on while Geller was concentrating and his badge doubled up!

I had also heard that in a recorded TV show in Sweden similar things happened, which led my brother David to demonstrate that you can record subtle energies on tape, video and audio, which replays successfully.

This is why we thought a healing broadcast might work in the same way, and why the listeners were encouraged to record it for later use as well. Indeed, afterwards, a stranger came to me and explained that his wife had been asleep during the programme. She had an inflamed leg. The following day he used the recording on her and she was healed. "All my friends are using it," he said. I know lots of people did record it.

Good heavens, I thought. We have created, with God's help, an icon on tape!

Miguel started to wind up the broadcast at 1.50am. "Where are you off to next?" he asked Magdalena and I. "Straight down to the airport to fly to Canada," I replied, and in an aside to Magdalena. "Just as well, we might just escape the lynch mobs."

We were back in Spain a week later. There was lots of mail. I never saw any of it. Miguel has asked for it to be sent to Rafael Coloma, he expressed himself delighted, and so were the programme directors. But I never obtained a strict analysis of the mail that they had received. They all seemed very happy at any rate.

143

I'm not sure what to make of it all, on the surface it worked, but I cannot put up a basic set of empirical data. I set it out, as something to be evaluated in other countries. I felt it worked, hopefully we'll learn more following that route.

Chapter 24

Individual Healing By Radio

In the December of 1990, I went to the Barcelona Healing Centre for a weekend seminar, and as was now the custom. Andreas Faber-Kaiser, author of "Jesus Lived and Died in Kashmir," invited me to his own two-hour programme on Radio Catalunya to "talk on healing"

By now, such talks were not as nerve wracking as at the beginning and I was fairly relaxed when I met him at the studio. Mabel and Brunni came with me to give moral support.

As he gave an initial summary of what spiritual healing was all about, a growing suspicion developed in my mind and it was confirmed when he invited members of the radio audience to phone in for individual healing!! An invisible hand reached into my stomach and grasped my entrails in a vice like grip. I knew I had always said that it was possible and I felt that one day I had to put it to the test, but I had not expected to be thrown into the deep end like this.

I had little time for reflection as the first caller suddenly came on the line. It was a case of "do or die" and on balance I thought that I had better "do" and called the insurance policy all healers have with the Holy Spirit.

It was a lady and the conversation went something like this.

"Hello. What is your name?"

"Rosel."

"What is the problem?"

"It is my skin. The Doctor says the cause is nervous and they cannot do anything for me."

"Well Rosel, this is the first time that I have done this on the radio, so please treat me gently and link yourself with me."

She agreed, and I started to look at her energies through the matchstick form.

There was attenuation in the limbs and a problem in the spine which she conceded. We got that right and I checked everything else which seemed in order and once again reminded her that it was the first time and it would be nice to meet her in person and have a little celebration. She agreed. I said that there was a chance that getting those energies right would resolve the problem.

Later, I did meet her and she said that she was much better.

And so, to the next and the next. It passed into a blur. Luckily, I have been given a recording of those two incredible hours. I have met two people who did receive healing, however, and they were both very pleased with the results.

One turned out to be the owner of a posh bar in Barcelona and he invited me there, insisting I went away with a bottle of Macallan Malt Whiskey. I had not the heart to refuse. (Ha!Ha!)

Thanks to God. It turned out to be a positive experience and I ended the programme involving all the listeners in a group healing whereby they sent healing to those whom they knew needed it.

Next day, there was a queue of some 30 people at the healing centre. It was great.

What was important was that I had survived the experience with some success and Andreas had dragged me through a psychological threshold I might not otherwise gone through voluntarily. For that I am grateful. It was also, to the best of my knowledge, another radio first and opens up all the new concepts about the true nature of consciousness very clearly and I hope it gives the confidence to other radio stations and other healers to do the same.

Ironically, when I returned three months later for a further broadcast. Andreas said, "You cannot do that anymore."

"Why not?" I said. "Have they banned healing by radio now?"

"No, it is not that. The stations policy is not to give personal consultations about anything. You can talk about healing, involve the audience, but you cannot deal with individuals. Nothing against healing, or you!"

I looked at him closely and he winked at me with a smile. "But we have proved it works, haven't we?

I laughed with him.

He put his arm around me and lead me into the studio where we did a programme on "The Templars and The Holy Grail" which was fascinating and the audience response was enormous.

Chapter 25

Jesus As Healer

One of the notable characteristics of Jesus was his ability to heal, and in any analysis of his healing acts, three main factors emerge:

1) That he forgave sins. (In the section on karmic healing, I have tried to deal with that.
2) That energy left him when he healed.
3) That he repeated very often, "Thy faith has made thee whole."
4) That he cast out devils.

I hope too, that I have made out a case that there is such an objective phenomenon as healing. When the woman who had a haemorrhage thanked him for healing, he knew that energy had left him.

But one may suppose that the whole issue of faith as being the faith in healing is what has provoked the notion of "healing" as being "faith healing". The popular notion of faith healing today is, so far as I am aware, something dramatic involving incantation and a form of emotional excitement, or at least it is so in some circles.

The casting out of devils always upsets people, and popular notions of exorcism with attendant films, have done nothing but surround the subject with either terror or disbelief.

I can only refer to the cases of schizophrenia, "voices", and the like that I mentioned earlier, and the case of the second energy body that contained an entity which I invited gently and undramatically to return to the "Source." I have had other cases of mental disturbance which have had the same apparent cause and have responded well.

There have also been cases of people attaching themselves to other, weaker people and draining their energy. It may be the source of vampire legends. Michael Bentine tells of one of these cases in a chapter of his book, "Doors of the Mind," with which I had to deal. It occurred in the South of France.

I consider it to be part of healing as well.

But all these things can be carried out in a loving, gentle, undramatic way. One needs total self-control and confidence, faith and the help of the Holy Spirit, but bell, book and candle can be forgotten.

Obviously, the extent to which the participants desire to be healed is significant and is, of course relevant. It is difficult for a healer even to deal with people who don't believe. They just don't come. So, the extent to which belief of faith is a factor is obviously something to be considered.

Matthew Manning is a great proponent of self-healing and has prepared various tapes for people to listen to in order to get themselves in the right state to create their own idea of their own wholeness.

But within the idea of faith lies the idea if will, of intent, of certainly, and elsewhere in this book I've tried to set out reasons why a healer or a sick person should never be surprised at a positive result. To be surprised you had to have doubt in the first place, and if you doubt in the first place, you don't have the absolute intent that is necessary. That's not to say one should be over-confident in healing, but at least dedicated to doing one's very best.

Failure to heal depends on two things, participation by the sick person, and the creation of a pure channel by the healer. Jesus was the purest of channels and represents a perfection to be aspired to rather than obtained. There is no record of Jesus failing to heal, except in his own village. No human healer has been able to claim such a thing, yet amongst healers, the healings of Jesus have been emulated, but never all by one person.

The other factor about Jesus is that energy left him when he healed, voluntarily or involuntarily, and at the very beginning I tried to show that consciousness, love energy, the stuff of the universe, the continuum in which the idea exists and from which it may manifest in the material, where archetypal concepts exist.

But it only happens where absolute intent, certainty or faith exists. Thus, in this context energy and faith must go hand in hand. In the world of the subtle energies there is little room for diffidence and doubt.

It is my contention that whereas Jesus was the Master Healer, we, as normal human beings, through a rational analysis of his healings, can develop a spiritual technique which may permit us at least to aspire to healing in a limited degree. As I said earlier, quite often simply boosting the basic energy of someone enables them to resolve their illness.

We can embark on this road in a rational way, knowing it has no end for us, but at least, on such of the journey was we may make, there are a great many things that we, in the healing mode may contribute.

I would go further and say that one day it is my warmest wish that healers are no longer treated as odd, separate, special beings, but their healing and the understandings involved are a universally shared attitude to ourselves, our neighbours, our community and the world.

Chapter 26

The Situation of Sins

I felt obliged to remark at the Conference in Madrid on "The Secret Life of Jesus", what is sin? The sins of the Anglican Church are in a different category from those of the Roman Church, although as a footnote to many who get very confused, the Anglican Church is Catholic and Apostolic, not Protestant as so many people erroneously think. It's just that it isn't Roman. We must look more closely at the true nature of sin.

The Romanisation of the Christian Church was instituted by the Emperor Constantine. Declared Emperor at York in England, sin of Queen Helen, believe it or not, of old King Cole of England, celebrated in nursery rhyme as a merry old soul, (merry means Mary).

Be all that as it may, what is sin? A lot of sins that didn't exist before were invented by the Church, and it's gone on inventing them as the centuries roll by. It's rather like the modern crime wave, contemporary society has created far more crimes to commit than there were a hundred years ago. Parking in the wrong place is a crime. It wasn't in the last century, it's relative crime now.

Not to believe in the Immaculate Conception, as far as I know, is a sin now, according to Roman theory, but it wasn't a hundred years or so. I hope they have retrospective absolution for those who were not aware they were sinning, just as the Mormons are into retrospective baptism, which is why they collect parish records from all over Europe and America. In order to baptise souls after death, all of which may be a good thing.

I cannot bring myself to believe that failure to subscribe to dogma that may vary with Popes and seasons is a terribly serious affair in the great scales of the last judgement. I do believe though, that there are acts which have repercussions on an individual, which may well affect his health.

Such sins are hatred, envy, pride, particularly pride of spirit, the most dangerous sin of all, that we think we are somehow better than others, and therefore have superior rights.

If you send out a malefic thought to another, if you wish him harm or downfall, then you are sinning. If you do not treat your neighbour in pure love, whatever harm he or she may do you, then you are sinning. If you unnecessarily harm any living thing for no good reason, then you are sinning. Even not to send love to your worst enemy is a sin.

Now there may be other sins written large in the great ecclesiastical book, but they are the sins of men against institutions. It's as serious as being a "Trot" in a Marxist community, or vice a versa. They are ephemeral, relative, humanist failings and the only retribution is man. "The only vengeance is mine," saith the Lord.

The way this works is that those malefic thoughts, whatever damage they may do to the person who is the object, certainly come winging back to the sender. Or so the theory goes. So when we thought about Jesus' healing by the forgiving of sins, it wasn't just a question of eliminating guilt feelings and trauma.

After the experience of karmic healing, we thought we'd have a look at the other energy bodies, where possibly the effect of such sins might lurk.

They're in the third energy body, and they're like warts or excrescences on that energy body, and when you clean them up, a new radiance pervades the person so affected, which they may maintain, so long as they have learned the lesson.

The absolution of sins is the sign of the cross, but I cannot believe it is simply a replica of the instrument of judicial execution. It's putting someone together again, laterally and vertically, clearing up their warts, and letting them know what's happening.

It's a tragedy of Western civilisation that the healing role of the priesthood is kept under wraps. Some poor parish priest in the West Country who held charismatic healing seances was even told by his bishop that it was alright as long as he kept it quiet.

It seems that the forgiving of sins of the present life is done that way, and the healers of the Aquarian Age may legitimately enter that field.

It is another thing to put on the check list.

If you have a good look at the sins of the various religions and cultures, they mostly concur in one thing, do no spiritual harm to your neighbour.

For the rest, I don't think God gets too upset. The great sin is failure to love your neighbour more than yourself, and many of those who don't may be recognised by dullness in their eyes.

As a footnote, I don't want to involve myself in some Anglican – Roman confrontation. It's just that it's the most talked about.

I had the great pleasure of meeting the Dalai Lama and I can't believe he would disagree with the forgoing definition of sin.

I do worry about priests who bless bombs and weapons. I do worry about churches which bless racism and white superiority. I was extremely worried about what went on in Nazi Germany, which seems to make Nietzchean will the summum bonum instead of love. See Nigel Pennick's book, "The Secret Sciences Of Hitler," published by Neville Spearman, with which I was involved.

I do not believe the doctrine of the Trinity has the least relationship to what has gone on in Ethiopia. That's a failure of love, although its ultimate resolution may not be to shower them with food. That is a short-term essential measure, but their problem reflects the original callousness of mankind.

Then there are, as the foregoing, the collective sins of the world. However convenient the national way of life may be for developed nationals, who by one way or another have avoided war with each other for some 45 years, there are collective sins against the third world nations, but that may be the subject of another book.

Chapter 27

Salamanca Story

Maria-Jesus said to me one day in 1984. "I'll arrange a lecture for you in Salamanca, where I live."

"OK," I said.

"I don't know how many will come."

"Well a dozen would be great."

Salamanca is a Spanish provincial city not far from the Portuguese border.

Some weeks later, I arrived in Salamanca.

"I've hired the theatre," she said, "I'll take you to see it." There we were a 400 seat modern auditorium.

"Well. It all seems a bit large, but we could all sit together in the front row," I said.

Next morning, together with Carmen, we went for a walk around the town. "By the way," said Carmen. "Here's the local radio station. We'll pop in and you can do a quick broadcast." And so it was, from the street to the beginning of a 20 minute interview about the night's lecture took about 5 minutes. It is better when it is spontaneous.

Then we continued our walk.

"Oh, here's a local newspaper office," said Carmen. "They want to do an interview, which duly appeared about 4pm.

Marie-Jesus said she'd had notices put up in the University. Salamanca boast one of the oldest universities in Europe.

We all came down to the theatre at 7.30pm, for the lecture was due to start at eight. Santiago was there, a Carmelite monk who had been on a course at the monastery of the Valley of the Fallen. He was to introduce me.

About 7.45pm a few people wandered in, and then a few more, there were about 20. "Not bad", I said, but they kept coming. All the seats were full, then they started to sit on the aisle steps and stand around against the walls. Suddenly the theatre was crammed to over-capacity. I was totally bemused as all at once there was I speaking to 600 Spaniards. Somehow it all worked. I showed at the end, how to use the hands to diagnose. A girl came up and took over the show, doing it immediately with volunteers on the stage.

In the event it was all a surprising success, and at the end I said that the following day in Santiago's convent up the road I would be pleased to give healing to anyone who needed it.

When I arrived, Santiago greeted me nervously.

"There are about 30 people upstairs," he said.

Well, there was nothing for it but to get on, so I did, particularly encouraging everybody to participate in giving energy, which they did.

Certain people, obviously, were going to need several treatments. I knew from experience that particularly in what I came to recognise as the Salamanca disease, namely arthritism, rheumatism, lumbago etc, one treatment was seldom enough, and so I promised to come back in a few weeks time.

Santiago seemed even more nervous.

"This time there are 40, it's incredible," he said.

I went for a walk in the main square at lunchtime, in which is a very beautiful monument, and suddenly a policeman put out his hand to stop me, as if I was a motor car. "Senor Bloy?" he asked. I nodded, wondering what on earth I had done or he thought that I had done. "I just want to thank you for healing my wife. I am the husband of Domi."

I recalled her. She had severe back trouble, and they had had to buy a ground floor flat as she could not go upstairs. Now she could and has played the normal role of the woman of a family ever since.

I was relieved.

"Muy bien," I said. "Pense que Usted Iba a arrestar-me!" – I thought you were going to arrest me! He laughed.

Domi became a good friend and helper to the group that was emerging. Later, she became a healer herself. So did Carmen, the other who took on the organisation.

Hence, I found myself committed to Salamanca once a month.

One day Carmen said she had had some sad news from Santiago. The Abbot had withdrawn permission for us to use the convent, saying that so many people were disturbing the peace of the convent, which was for God's work.

"That's telling us!" I said, whereupon Tito, who was a manufacturing tailor, immediately put his workshop at our disposal. There was an enormous cutter's table about the length of a cricket pitch, and when the word got about more, there were queues out into the street. A new Abbot came to the convent and invited us back, but we felt comfortable with Tito.

One day, two years later, Jenni, Lisa and Pasqualine had come for the week at the Valley of the Fallen. I asked them over for the day at Salamanca, which was just as well as during the day 160 people came. We just got through by 10.30pm and they all shared the load.

"Look," I said to Carmen. "We can't continue like this."

She agreed and sadly we had to limit the numbers to 50 per visit, and tickets were issued, (not sold.) She never confined it to 50, but it did not matter. People protested when they did not get one.

It was all quite extraordinary. Everybody came, from all walks of life, simple country folk from surrounding villages, priests, one of whom tried to pretend he wasn't, doctors, business men, housewives, babies and children. I think I got to see every type of degenerative illness at close quarters.

I let it be known very firmly that this was sacred work and I wanted no money or gifts, but I could not refuse the occasional bottle of wine, or jar of honey that people brought from their villages. It was very moving, and joyous because I always tried to promote laughter rather than sobriety.

I cannot say what the success rate has been. I know of several who did not get any benefit. I know of one or two who died of their advanced conditions soon afterwards. I know of many who came back just to say thank you, or some who would come back and say they had something or other, whom I remembered from months back with disappointment.

"Oh, you didn't get any benefit from the treatment," I would say.

"Oh, yes," they would reply. "I was healed of what I had then. This is a new problem." And of course, as I said earlier, healers tend to get the hopeless cases, and have a tough job statistically.

People would wave in the street and come over to say thank you, and of course new people kept coming. There was no advertising, just word of mouth.

It's really impossible for me to say more than this for it has been an incredibly positive experience. But I have never been able to keep track of the cases, so I have asked Carmen to write a summary of what she feels the results in Salamanca have been to date, four years later, and I do hope that a professional investigative journalist will one day try to evaluate what has happened there.

Then I met Magdalena, and she started to come to Salamanca with me.

Magdalena is a naturist, a natural healer and a very gentle soul, particularly with animals and humans who are in need.

She added a new dimension to it all. I will not anticipate anything she will tell in her biography about her experiences in Hungary and Russia as a pressed KGB agent, but from her grandmother she learned a lot about herbalism. She survived the KGB's ministrations as a whole human being. After being tortured as a punishment for trying to escape, she was immediately put on the EEG and her brain rhythms monitored. To the surprise of the doctor, they were totally normal.

"After what you have been through," he said. "I would not expect the toughest soldier to have such a brain pattern.

The point is that due to the many sufferings and tragedies in her life, which can either make or break a person, she learned total self-control, and that is crucial in healing, the control of consciousness.

Now I had been healing in a technical sense under pressure. I always made a point of making personal eye contact, joking with the person, berating them if I thought that they needed it, but it was never enough.

Magdalena began to weed out people after my healings she thought she could help specifically and would spend half an hour or more with individuals advising them particularly on diet. No meat or fish, how to clean their bodies by right eating and drinking, listening to their problems, and so on. She could feel and give energy from the first day that we met. I only needed to tell her that it existed.

Then when they returned, they go straight to her, and leave me out, unless she instructed them otherwise. Roman, Tito's brother, who helped organise as well, put his arm around me with a smile one day and said. "Magdalena gets better results than you."

"I'm so pleased," I said.

"The point is she is counselling people who need it, and you don't have time to."

I was delighted.

Now some may say I must have had a pang of jealousy. I can honestly say I felt nothing but pleasure, and healers should never be competitive. If you know another healer gets best results with certain conditions, send the person there. I always step aside when another healer is there who can help.

Now in case you think this is a form of inverted ego, it arises from the simple technical observation that if you want to be a healer, forget your ego. I want to be a healer. My ego can come out in other ways, if it wants to.

Apart from that Magdalena and I had decided to team up for life, and heal together, so it was good news on a purely sentimental level.

On Magdalena's second visit in came a young man in the wheelchair that I mentioned earlier, who had come the month before. This time he came in walking and went straight over to Magdalena and kissed her.

What Magdalena's arrival in my life did was to show me that counselling, diet and healing should go hand in hand. That was good. It was then I got up a dummy visiting card which said:

We have the honour to tell you that you
Have just received healing from a former
Member of the KGB and a former member of
British Counter-Intelligence.

"A NEW SERVICE TO HUMANITY"

We had a good laugh together, but never dared show it to anyone, but of course it's ironically true.

The whole Salamanca episode, which is only just beginning, was unexpected, but I did see we might have been steered into a commitment where something important was to be learned. Now four years later, Carmen and Domi are into healing and counselling and others are following.

Although there is absolutely no charge, we did invite contributions to buy proper surgery couches, for getting old ladies on the cutter's tables was a dangerous and risky procedure. Magdalena was most unhappy at this, but I said there was no question of not healing anyone who didn't contribute. What I felt was right that they should buy the equipment for themselves, and start to become a self-help group which might one day form a healing and counselling centre staffed by Salamancans. That would be the proper ending to our visits. There was no way that we could keep visiting Salamanca forever, but creating healers and counsellors there was the most laudable objective and logical conclusion.

Chapter 28

Our Own Pharmacy

Someone once said that whatever doctors might do, a significant majority of sick people get better anyway – the body heals itself. Indeed, it is arguable that what is called health is keeping illness at bay. The body is always producing cancerous cells, the liver has an inevitable tendency towards cirrhosis, etc, and this may be true.

What determines health is that the idea of our perfection, the original blueprint, (may be the cross of triangles), remains in command and orders back into the line the rogue elements that constantly manifest. We have seen elsewhere that this is a question of morale, of remaining interested in living, and an essential part of healing is re-establishing the desire to live, it may be waking the person up to the realities of spiritual man, of making life worth living on the basis that we recognise the divine spark within us, not just because we enjoy material conveniences in life. Learning to love is of course, the fundament of it all, and to that extent, the healer may work successfully in the awakening of consciousness and the harmony of chakras.

A prime cause of cancer is stress, simply that life just isn't worth living, and thus the subtle forces that keep a body healthy have no sustenance.

Now, whereas it is evident to healers that mankind is mind, body and spirit, that is not to say that our body is not a complex of chemical balances and interactions in the first instance.

In recent years, the ability of the body to produce endorphins that remove pain has become a recognised phenomenon. What other medicaments does the brain also produce and what might it be able to produce if other conditions are correct.

As I mentioned earlier, Matthew Manning's tapes which encourage the visualisation of white cells devouring rogue cells are effective. Thus, we may enquire as to the limits of such a process. If we accept these propositions, one may presume that a person who lives a full healthy life may have the brain to produce whatever medication the body needs to remain healthy, totally regulated consciously or unconsciously.

It has recently occurred to me to look for the archetypal form in the brain of a fully functioning pharmacy, and was shown a 64 line sun wheel, with a loop at each point.

Chapter 29

Self-Healing

It is open to discussion, that if disease has subtle causes, to do with trauma, sin – as defined earlier, karmic, genetic causes, etc, as to whether the key to healing is not within the gift of the unfortunate sufferer.

Of course, that must be true, in the last analysis. But often, in the first analysis, the sufferer is involved in a form of closed circuit, where he or she may even positively want to die.

A good friend, a senior practitioner in cancer diagnosis and therapy, readily stated to me that in a given group of cancer sufferers with identical symptoms and conditions, some might succumb rapidly, some have a significant ensuing life span, and some might have a "spontaneous remission" – a term which I take to be a cop-out by the medical profession in order not to face up to the fact that their metaphysical model of reality might not be adequate. My friend's honest question was, "What is the difference between these groups? What is the critical factor?" For that reason, he has much interested himself in alternative medicine.

In my conversations with Jung and his discarnate associates, the point they always made about cancer was that it wasn't just a question, as in the impetigo incident, of gently inviting the archetypal form to depart. There was much more to it than that. Cancer in spite of certain viral aspects, was a much more complex and subtle condition. It also raised the question as to whether the sufferer really wanted to live.

Of course, you can deliberately expose yourself to carcinogenic agents ie, tobacco, inadvertently asbestos, certain petrochemicals and so on. But even so, there are differences, some succumb, some don't. Some workers in nuclear installations suffer, some don't. What's the difference? What can the healer or sufferer do? There are those who say that cancer is latent in all of us. Advanced cancer therapies tend towards the idea of stimulating the body's natural resources in favour of a more active destruction of cancer cells, rather than hitting the body with radio/chemotherapy. To me, it implies there is a breakdown in the plan of our original perfection in any event.

Now the healer may do his best to reverse those factors in cancer which tend to be either chemical or viral by visualisation or energy channelling – and/or look for improvements in awareness or trauma and so on, but above all, the greatest intervention he can make is to hand back the responsibility to the sufferer.

Now those who have given in to their condition clearly need not only the stimulus of the healing energy in their organisms, but also the conviction that there is something they themselves can do to improve their condition, there are also those who have decided to die and have a form of self-induced cancer because they have effectively given up living, and have therefore withdrawn from the idea of their basic perfection the energy that sustains it, not necessarily deliberately, but at all events subconsciously.

Now once again the obvious ethical problem poses itself – has a healer the right to impose something on somebody against their will? My answer to that has always been that healing is about loving and there is no cosmic law against that, in fact, it is the contrary. Indeed, making death sweet is a great healing, so it isn't necessarily a life prolonging imposition.

But the whole question of consciousness enters into the equation. Is the difference between survivors and succumbers is one of consciousness? For those who have made a decision to die, would they change that decision if they were more aware of the spiritual realities? And given the fact that spiritual realities are not necessarily comprehended intellectually, but through heightened perception then perhaps the healer through the techniques discussed can help raise the perceptions so that they may wish to reverse that decision. Now if that is the case, it is very difficult, if not impossible for the individual to escape from their closed circuit without a healer. At least, we should assist the sufferer to have a totally clear perception of what is really happening in order, a) to decide to reverse the decision and b) consciously to participate in their subsequent healing in their own account.

Now none of this is to say that if someone really consciously decides to die in complete awareness, they are doing something wrong. Indeed, in those circumstances there is nothing the healer could do any way. The Cathars deliberately chose to die in certain special circumstances.

For those who have conditions induced by external factors, and who only need the information, and for those who have reversed their decision to die, this does not of course, uniquely apply to cancer, there is a lot that the individual can do to carry his or her own healing further.

The healer's function is a) to wake up, b) to channel basic energy and archetypal healing and c) to inform the sufferer how to proceed, given, then, the desire to live has been established. Just as the healer is trying to re-establish the original idea of perfection of the individual in the mind, body and spirit. Goethe's *Urfplanze*, God's original idea of you. The individual can work on that, too, by disciplining himself to re-establish that idea in his own consciousness.

Some counsel the regular visualisation in a meditative state of a bright blue light that enters through the head and sweeps all parts of the body like a broom pushing in front of itself an increasing pile of black specks like dust, and finally expelling it all through the feet into the earth, leaving the body clean and vibrant.

But above all else, the re-establishment of the joy of living in full consciousness is the most critical factor, not in a facile, shallow way, but in the very real, sense that the human being, in full awareness, is in God's image, not in the sense that God is humanoid, but in a sense that we may mirror to a greater extent than we may realise what may be known as Cosmic Consciousness, and that should never be disposed of except for a very good reason indeed.

Now it may not be that our bodies are glamourous, well-functioning organisms capable of winning beauty competitions – it may well live in a wheelchair or limited to bed. What about Stephen Hawking? Or what about a young man in the South of France, virtually totally immobile due to muscular dystrophy, yet healing others until the last day of his sadly brief life. That is what is meant by being alive and embodying the divine spark. I had the joy and privilege of knowing him. Those who believe it to be other, I humbly submit, remain asleep.

For the healer to wake people up, stimulate their centres, their perceptions, their organisms, is to hand back to the individual the responsibility for their own health and set them free to heal themselves – thus self-healing finds it's own level.

When community healing has raised the collective level of consciousness, then the healer will no longer be a special person – not that he is now for those who understand, but gently fade into the wider background of a generally agreed and comprehended scenario about the nature of spiritual reality, and they will no longer stick out from the background.

All that having been said, however, all people can get themselves into states of depression or trauma, which is a closed circuit, out of which another person may be the only instrument of restoring them once again to self - reliance and self - comprehension.

Chapter 30

Sickness and Family

Something I was taught very early in in this adventure, I think by Joyce Netchek, to whom I owe much, was that many conditions of ill health have their origins amongst the family of the sufferer. This, of course, is a matter of some obviousness, and may be seen to be so by many of us in our experience of non-subtle realities of family life.

It therefore follows, especially in cases where trauma is evident – closing of the heart chakra and evidence in the second energy body – that healers would do well not just to help that person individually, but to have a look through the archetypes, of other members of the family.

There is a family ethos, an *egregore*, as well, which needs healing. It is, I think, a truism that families may be very happy or very miserable. Those families whose prime movers understand the reality of love, the real sort, are fortunate, but there are many where the prime movers are either totally frustrated that their progeny do not conform to their pre-conceived ideas of what life is about, and seek to impose them in inappropriate circumstances. For example, making one's son be a Royal Marine, when it just isn't his scene, or deploring a desire of a child to play Rugby for England when one hoped for a romantic poet, there is a sort of genetic and karmic lottery in it all. There is also the traumatised parent having a contagious effect on the unfortunate progeny, (I'm not referring in any way to genetic abnormalities here.)

It's not just from parents to children, it can be the other way around.

A lady came to me with a beaten-up heart chakra, and when I asked who had done it, with relieving tears she eventually said it was her father in childhood. "Have you forgiven him?" I asked. No, came the reply.

I asked her to do so and her eventual joy was wonderful to behold after she had completed the act of forgiveness. There are more subtle effects of the family *egregore* upon us. Indeed, it's not so long ago that the karma of mankind was based on the family. It says so in the Bible, and the sins of the father shall be visited on the sons and daughters until the seventh generation. In the Age of Aquarius, it's potentially different. Individuals who wake up take on the responsibility, knowingly and lovingly for their neighbour, and the genetic family basis has eroded in favour of the spiritual family, which is all mankind, but those members of genetic families who have made that transition can make a most loving contribution to the improvement of the *egregore* of their genetic family.

Once again, we enquired as to whether there was an archetype of that *egregore*.

(Edge forming a circle)

Maria-Asunta found this a bit difficult and has come to an arrangement with the collective consciousness to simplify the archetype into a line of 64 bars.

She applies it to the family as a whole, and to individual members.

It is also becoming plain that a blocked heart chakra, or any other, affects the general flow of vital energy around the body, thus affecting organs as well. It may well manifest as a blockage in the spine and should not be confused with an organic spinal problem.

When recently, a sad but sweet 18-year-old girl came for healing at a meeting near Salisbury, and her heart chakra was closed, I had the opportunity to look at the family archetype and found it with parts missing. In suggesting to her that the cause was in the family, she immediately agreed, and the tears flowed, which was good for her and helped us to learn more.

Chapter 31

Healing and Doctors

I have made earlier references to the fact that certain trials on placebos have shown that some doctors get better results than others, with or without placebos, and I am totally satisfied that there are doctors who practice healing, consciously or unconsciously.

Recently a most significant advance was made in Britain. Whereas any patient has a right to invite a healer to treat them in hospital, it is now open to GP's under new legislation to send patients, who remain under supervision, to complementary practitioners, this includes spiritual healers.

When my mother some years ago had abandoned all hope of her diverticulitis improving, she went into hospital for removal of a section of her intestine. While she was resting in the pre-med state, I started to boost her vital fields in preparation, when in walked her G.P. "Here comes trouble," I thought. "You're Colin, aren't you?" he said. "I know what you are doing. I send patients to healers sometimes." We had a very pleasant chat.

As a matter of interest, I was in the ward when my mother returned. She had no vital energy at all, and I speedily set about restoring it. She made a good recovery.

Of course any doctor who sends a patient to a healer remains responsible, and will generally need to know that a professing healer is a subscriber to the code of conduct of a reputable healing organisation, although I do have to say that those who retain in their codes a prohibition on the treatment of venereal disease really should bring them up to date.

It goes without saying that neither spiritual healing or conventional medicine can do everything. They can't. But the opportunities to work together should be created to get the best of both worlds.

I can think of no clinical condition which should not be the legitimate objective of healing, and I can think of no case where a healer should seek to influence a sick person not to consult with their doctor.

I remember a case in Barcelona of a young man whose sinus canals were closing and whose doctor said he would need a somewhat unpleasant operation. He asked for my help and I performed an operation on the etheric level, pushing my finger down the canals to open them wider. "Should I see the doctor again?" "Of course," I replied. He came back a month later and said that to his doctor's surprise there had been an improvement, and he would no longer need the operation. He thanked me profusely. "It's nothing." I replied. "I'm just glad it wasn't haemorrhoids!"

There is another doctor in Barcelona whom I do not know, but refers in various lectures to incidents involving children in coma. One girl, a 12yr old, was given up as irremediable, and I went to the hospital with Maria-Asunta and Maria-Carmen. We were able to enter the area, but we could only observe through a plate glass window. She was being examined by the doctor, who saw us. There was nothing for it but to do the business in spite of his presence.

I stimulated the labyrinth of consciousness, the chakras, the brain, nervous system etc, etc, etc when I looked up he was no longer there and I forgot about it.

On my next visit, there was a baby of a few months who had fallen on her head, and was similarly affected and abandoned as irremediable. We worked on her from a distance at first. She started to improve, then we were able to visit her in the children's hospital, where the improvement was evident. Later she recovered completely.

Now this doctor apparently tells the story about both cases, saying there is some weird Englishman who waves his hands around in an extraordinary way, and people in comas come out. I must meet him one day if I can find him.

Actually, I have treated many cases of coma, and they have all proved positive.

Reminder to Reader: When I say "I" you know what I mean – see Contract With Holy Spirit, at the back of the book.

People who are receiving chemotherapy improve with healing as it helps counter the negative effects of the treatment. One must keep the vital energy levels high, chemotherapy saps them, but that is no reason for suggesting chemotherapy is wrong. Similarly, AIDS drugs have a sapping effect, and should be supplemented by healing.

Antibiotics are similar. In some cases, the post-treatment depression is worse than the illness it "cured". Healing should go hand in hand with all forms of surgery, medication, psychotherapy, physiotherapy etc, etc, but it would be much nicer if more people went to a healer early on, even on a regular basis like one goes to a dentist, for prevention is better than cure, and many people still come to a healer in search of miracles, a therapy of last resort, (which is nice if it works,) but as we have said earlier, the duty of healers is to avoid miracles ever being necessary.

One of the difficulties of modern medicine is that they only use a positivist model of reality. No account of energy bodies, chakras, spirit, not to mention archetypes is taken, nor reincarnation.

To say to someone as a G.P. that they may have karmic problems is therefore impossible. To suggest that they may not have incarnated completely unthinkable. Yet for all I know the Chairman or President might go to church regularly, many doctors do, and one is bound to presume they do recognise a spiritual dimension to reality, so why not apply the same criteria to medicine?

It would be most helpful if a model based on spiritual man rather than merely electrical-chemical were put in place.

The wider implications of healing go far beyond therapy, they concern the healing of the collective consciousness of our species, that finally it really learns to love, and thereby save the planet.

Chapter 32

Healing and Modern Medicine

Jean-Claude Seconde, a good friend of yesteryear looked between conventional doctors and practitioners of alternative therapies, to find common ground. During one session, one, dedicated obsessively to healing, felt obliged to heckle a medical doctor who was speaking denouncing all modern medicine in a tirade, proclaiming that we had no need of it.

As he was in a wheelchair, with which I sympathised, Jean-Claude had him wheeled out and banned him from the rest of the conference, with which I also sympathised.

Now Madame Blavatsky, in one of her essays, quotes another as saying. "Now here is the history of Occult Sciences in a nutshell. 1) Once known, 2) Lost, 3) Rediscovered, 4) Denied, 5) Re-affirmed."

Which is about right except the word "occult" is suspect. Which is why Rudolph Steiner spoke of Spiritual Science.

Now the history of mankind is a curious faltering, stuttering affair, of steps backwards and forwards, and the argument as to whether mankind has progressed in any way in recorded history is open to discussion as to where we may be at the moment, if indeed some form of linear progression exists, this is highly questionable. I happen to be an optimist on a good day.

I cannot ally myself with those who reject modern medicine. Indeed I have every sympathy with those who feel themselves called as doctors in this day, and age, and are more or less bound to accept the world view that is the bedrock of current medical thinking, although, one is bound to say, things really are improving, and healers ought to be only too well aware that, by no means, can they achieve all that they would like to, and, at the same time, doctors know that sometimes there are cures that they cannot explain and have causes outside their frame of reference.

"Spontaneous remission" is a way of explaining self-healing of cancer. The thought that they ought to investigate why it happens never seems to occur. It is put in its compartment and they get on with the conventional wisdom. In the same way, museum curators describe artefacts that don't fit the current view of things as "anomalies". Well, I ask you. It's the one that gets away that tells the truth. Thus, Heisenberg exploded Newtonian particle theory.

But at the end of the day the human condition, this "vale of tears", has many problems to cope with, not least our own version of truth.

There is a bit of an alliance between healers and herbalists, as if they are in the same business, but so far as I can see if that alliance holds water, then so should an alliance with modern medicine, which uses naturally occurring drugs and their derivatives when they are relevant. What's an aspirin? A derivative of a natural product of the willow tree, now it is used to prevent heart attacks.

We are all committed, if we set aside glory and renown, to the healing of illness. The problem is, as I see it, that modern medicine has a wrong mode of the nature of man.

Now if you have an infected wound, a broken leg, a bad appendix, varicose veins, and so on, modern medicine does a very good job, which is not intended to be patronising, but it is all based on a superficial view of man's nature.

And wherever there's suggestion that there might be something else, well, dump that with psychology and psychiatry, and look at the disasters the unfortunate pseudo-science has created. Granted certain mental disorders are based on physical conditions, which may be corrected by simple drugs and surgery, but it has become an area in which the worst abuses of medical experiment have been and are being perpetuated, all under the guise of "medicare", yet one would imagine the animal rights lobby would go "nuclear." If they really understood what was going on in the psychiatric clinics of today in the name of human medicine.

It's not the fault of the psychiatrist, it is because the model of humanity they follow does not admit of the spiritual reality of mankind, and they do not create the model.

The model, I submit, was created by the following list of sinners in our era:

1) The Emperor Constantine for politicising Christianity, and the Christian bishops for agreeing.
2) The Medieval Church for creating the Inquisition when other versions of the truth arose.
3) Auguste Comte for suggesting the philosophy of logical positivism.
4) Those who suppressed the rest of what Newton and Descartes wrote.
5) Sigmund Freud for implying that the libido is the only motivating force.
6) Charles Darwin, who published against his better nature.
7) Karl Marx for dialectical materialism.

8) Pavlov for the conditioned reflex, and all the other time-servers and fellow travellers who didn't have the courage to rock the boat when they knew better. The one that gets away is conveniently ignored, when it's the one that has the truth. In a sense we are all guilty.

I suppose we should also have a list of saints:

1) The nameless who protested and whose views were never heard.
2) All heretics who never practised hate.
3) Those in the church who first escaped the charge of heresy – Raimund Llull, St John of the Cross, Paracelsus, to name but three.
4) The French Romantic and Symbolist poets.
5) Francis Bacon.
6) Albert Einstein, a supremely religious man.
7) Rudolf Steiner, a prophet of the 20th century.
8) Carl Gustav Jung, for his perception of the collective consciousness.
9) and apologies to so many others not on the list.

It is a hollow exercise but it may give some sort of background to the historical influences that have determined the current positivist/agnostic view of man which pervades our sociology, economics, political and above all medical attitudes.

All of which places modern medicine in a difficult position, and those who would like to escape have problems.

Chapter 33

The Objects Of Healing

There is a great danger that healers see themselves as miracle workers. I believe, as I said earlier, that the primary duty of a healer is to make miracles unnecessary, just as the primary duty of a doctor is to make preventative medicine his first obligation. Maintaining people in a good state, so that they don't get ill is of primary importance.

I remember a friend who was so keen to do miracles, he sought out sick people. I believe that to be wrong. If they come your way, then obviously you do your best, but to seek to do miracles above all else is wrong.

That is why I chose the title, "I'm just going down to the pub to do a few miracles," as a throw away phrase, because the real miracles are the undramatic ones, simply preventing illness.

I recognise that this is not an attitude of mind generally shared by humanity though it is perhaps not that far away. Helping your neighbours keep in good health, in mind, body and spirit is undramatic, but critically important and the best thing that you can do. Maybe if this book gains wide enough currency, people will understand that this is what it's really all about. Perhaps this is the ideal aspect of the future.

Let's look at healing as it currently stands. Mostly, people who come to healers are in their extremity. It is a matter of last recourse. I believe that healers as a group must seek, in the first instance, to show that they can assist orthodox medicine in ways I have outlined before. That's for the moment, helping existing drug therapies, assisting in reducing operational shock, and so on.

All that is to do with the physical symptoms of the body. But once you have got the hands going, you are in a position to analyse problems in the etheric body, sort them out before they manifest in the physical, re-align the etheric with the physical where trauma and physical shock has taken their toll. You can organise the five geometrical forms which have an archetypal function. It's undramatic. You can heal the Karma there's not much credit in it, but that doesn't matter. Where an apparent miracle is necessary, OK, do it. It may work. It may not, but at the end of the day, making them unnecessary is the crucial factor. One day we're all going to shed this mortal coil, and healers can do more than anyone to make old age and dying more agreeable.

I have the belief that to die happy and in full consciousness is a blessing. Healers can help people to do this. Healer's die too. They are ordinary mortals. John Leslie died of cancer, but he died in full awareness. To make death sweet is another fundamental obligation of the healer.

I repeat that miracles are the thing that healers must seek to avoid at all costs, and not seek to demonstrate.

Now I have done what others call miracles and I hope that I have explained that really it was very simple, giving basic energy, aligning chakras, etc.

However, there is something I must make totally clear. I do not heal as a form of imposition, the notable successes I have had are not because I am a special person. They are because I have been able to release or unblock within a person the energies that needed to flow to activate his own ability to heal himself.

That having been said, one is faced with the problem of false ego or excessive ego.

Healers don't heal. They are the channel that permits healing to take place. They are lucky chaps to have that privilege. Yes, one may say, "I am a good channel", I suppose that's ego, on one level. But it all comes back to the beginning of this tale, self-awareness! That's all. The extent to which one is self-aware, and recognises the third ego state, is the extent to which you can heal. The extent to which you are not yet self-aware, is the extent to which you have not realised yourself, that's not a big deal. To realise yourself is simply to learn to love, and I must quote the Christian creed here, to "love without hope of any rewards save that of knowing that we do Thy will." That's all there is folks. Self-realisation, self-fulfilment, self-completion. And shut up! You don't have to tell others about it other than to share.

Chapter 34

The Role of Ego

I had the idea of leaving two blank pages for this chapter, but on reflection, it would have created the wrong impression.

I hope that I have made it clear that any healer who thinks that he or she may have healed someone without any outside aid is on a fast, downhill journey, but, of course that does not imply that the ego has no role in healing.

At the end of the day, every healer has a style, his or her way of doing things, indeed not all results were uniquely achieved by the "correct" application of the rules of spiritual science. In theory, and in practice, you can heal someone without a gesture or a change of expression. That's how it is when you work alone and at a distance. It is all in the mind and the spirit, and the total dedication of all you've got to the visualisation.

You can also heal with a smile, with an embrace, let someone cry things out of them, sometimes speak sharply to them if they need a jolt, and quite a few do. That's all the power of suggestion and, of course, many medical people dismiss the results of healing in this way. "It's all suggestion."

Well, if you can suggest away someone's cancer, (which actually you can in certain cases), or headaches or any other condition, isn't it about time the phenomena were understood and used by doctors, much more than it is, and of course, good, caring doctors will take time out to implant such a suggestion, such time as the present constitution of the NHS permits, (actually I have a feeling that if all doctors took more time and had a more loving approach at first interview, the total time and resource devoted to the patient in the long run would be less. It would be worth a study by the BMA, at least they conceded that's how alternative practitioners get their results.)

If they are, as healers, to use the power of suggestion, and we certainly should, you don't have to prove that spiritual healing works every time you make someone feel better, then we do need to use our personalities.

Now some would maintain that a person who has successfully "killed their ego", as they would have it, have established the essential pre-condition for achieving spiritual wonders. With experience, I have become most suspicious of this approach, and I often wonder if it isn't another name for spiritual narcissism, or pride of spirit, an odious sin, the worst according to some.

We need our egos to create the right conditions for suggestion, indeed to create the right conditions for healing. The pre-match warm up is all important for both.

Thus, the smile, the touch, the joke, the clear look are all tools of the trade, but false warmth is self-defeating. What makes up our ego, or personality, is something that should be at our disposal when we need it, and set to one side when we don't, and that when we are doing the visualisations that are the key to spiritual healing. That's where love comes in, a very personal discipline to secure the good of the outer person.

That's when every fibre, atom, particle, wave and essence of our being is deliberately concentrated on the formation of the new image of perfection of the sick person, the affected organ or whatever. It's the time when what we might be doing at the weekend, what the news of the day might have been, whether the cat is pregnant and so on, is set aside. They are the business of the banal, mundane ego, and that has no place in healing.

Don't kill your ego, keep it in a drawer for when you need it, and set it aside when you don't.

Back to Paul Valery. "Je me Voyais me voir." "I saw myself look at myself." From the star chakra observe yourself, warts and all, that's how you know yourself. Let your ego be your friend and ally, not your master. From the high point of consciousness, consciously use it when you need to.

Please don't kill it, it adds variety and spice to life. Treat it as you would a theatrical mask in medieval theatre, never cynically but lovingly aware of the needs of others when it is appropriate.

All of which having been said, it is still not good enough to content oneself with the comforting idea that one is a good manipulator of the mundane self, the truth is when we operate from the new higher chakras, we are not ourselves anyway, we are deliberately combining ourselves with a pool of consciousness which is not our own, but which we may have the privilege of bringing to bear on an act of healing. The extent to which one does that may well be a source of fulfilment, but never of pride.

But I do remember once making a lot of runs against a powerful Australian team, which included test match players, and I was proud of that. That is of course different, but I do have the pleasure in telling you about it, I that's the mundane ego – and of course I told you deliberately to illustrate a point. Or did I?

Chapter 35

Should healers be paid?

Anyone who dedicates themselves to healing and has no other form of income has to charge for their services. They must keep themselves fed and clothed, and may well have duties to their families.

There is a code of ethics laid down by the National Federation of Spiritual Healers which is useful. Healers I know around Europe have a fixed charge per "patient", (I don't like the word,) irrespective of the time they spend, and those who are waiting, just have to wait. Of course, no haler should ever deter anyone who cannot, or possibly will not pay, and they should be quite clear about this. But at the same time, they are quite entitled to suggest to the better off people that they make a donation on top to cover those who cannot pay.

Clearly, healers should accept that they are not in the business to do more than secure reasonable living standards for themselves and their families. Champagne and caviar, so to speak, are to be avoided.

Naturally, if you are in a comfortable economic position anyway, then you have the privilege of being able to give healing. I have been in that fortunate position, and so long as it lasts, I will never have to accept money or anything other than a friendly token of thanks, like a bottle of home-made wine.

I repeat, a healer with no other income is entitled to charge and should feel no qualms whatever in doing so, so long as those who cannot afford it are never denied healing.

Chapter 36

What is healing?

It is healing from the spirit, through the spirit, to the spirit.

It is the creation by one person, the healer, in the purest of consciousness, of the thought form of the perfection of the person who is ill, and sending it to his spirit through the ultimate continuum, pure consciousness.

Pure consciousness is pure love, is pure energy.

Those who wake up in consciousness may participate in further evolution and creation.

Thus, they may assist in healing individuals, communities, nations and our planet.

Pure Love Is Pure Spirit

Both Are All.

Chapter 37

Look For The Subtle Cause First

Whereas in the beginning there was a natural tendency to look first at the physical body and seek to put that right immediately, and there was much success, the understanding of the outer energy bodies, the genetic code, karma, etc, imposes a different discipline, which is, except in obvious cases of broken bones, injections and the like, to look for a potential subtle cause before doing anything.

A typical case might be of someone with a heart problem. One looks at the first energy body and finds a weakness around the heart area. Next, one checks the archetype of the heart – it is not correct. Checking out the blood, the nervous system, the endocrine system, etc, do we find possibly related causes there? Go through the check list. Is there something in the other energy bodies, the chakras etc? Make a note of what isn't right. The genetic code, the cross, the triangles – is there a karmic problem? Do nothing until the whole check list is complete.

When you have been through everything we currently understand, then act appropriately with the must subtle of the defects noted and work your way backwards through the list. Putting the karma right may put all the noted anomalies in order, or some. It helps the healer understand the true cause.

Of course, it may be that it is just a bad heart, and one has helped other things at other levels, but to leave action until a full analysis has been carried out may well produce a more satisfactory healing, because we may explain to the person something of critical importance to their general well-being rather than send them home with a good heart and totally over awed by the powers of the individual healer.

More and more I realise, and very much due to Maria-Asunta, that the most effective and valuable aspect of healing is the healing of consciousness and the spirit. It is the most important dimension of spiritual healing, and is more relevant than ever with the shift of group consciousness that it is evident the world is undergoing, there is a mutation of consciousness – Homo Sapiens has the ability to mutate to Homo Amans. It is the Karma of all those who wake up, be they professed healers or not, to help those asleep to heal not only their bodies, but their spirits.

Chapter 38

Healing Plants

We used to do some experiments in various monasteries with plants that looked a bit sickly. That was in the early days of removing their etheric bodies to one side, simply to practise the phenomenon. We always left them with more vital energy, they were always more vigorous the following day.

At the same time, we would encourage people to give energy to plants simply to persuade them that they could do it to human beings.

When a sickly plant had been chosen, it was curious to see that after the first experiment, the plant would co-operate with us, reducing its energy so that the next person could come and practise.

It seemed a complete confirmation of Clive Baxter's work.

Once you establish this form of contact with plants, they flourish. Anyone who wishes can come and see my crazy philodendron, or my great yucca, the basil plants and so on. They are incredible.

When I was in Tenerife some years ago, Emilio Bourgon and his friends took me to their experimental orchard on the side of Teide volcano. They had deliberately evoked energies of devas around the fruit trees, which were flourishing. I was able to dowse their fields and the fact that there was a circle around each one. I remembered what Michael Bentine has said about Amazon Indians pre- germinating their seeds in circles of earth. I also saw Bill Lewis, the Welsh wizard, healing trees.

To me, it shows how the human being should relate to his plants and trees. Prince Charles is a very serious and informed gentleman. We can safely say that the agri-business is a real phenomenon of the wasting of an irreplaceable assets.

In the New Age, just as at Findhorn, real agriculture must take into account real and invisible ecology, and of Steiner's bio-dynamic system and the whole question of giving energy to plants just as one does to human being, but just as one would advise a human being as to diet, so the proper cultivation of plants and crops must take into account proper diet.

The simple experiment of putting mustard and cress in a wet towel and giving energy to one side and not the other is something anyone can do to demonstrate the difference without shadow of a doubt.

Just as T Hieronymous Galen irradiated fields at a distance and freed them from pests, healing in an agricultural sense can do a lot towards creating a productive ecological balance in the bio-system.

Chapter 39

The Holy Spirit and its role in Healing

Many readers will be familiar with the passage in St Paul's epistle which deals with spiritual gifts. He says there are varieties of gifts but the same spirit, and in each of us the Spirit is manifested in a particular way, for a particular purpose. He includes the gift of prophecy, to distinguish true spirits from false, the gift of ecstatic utterance, which I take to mean mediumship, and miraculous powers, and healing.

(1 Corinthians 12 et seq.)

You may wonder why the Church has had so much difficulty with its healing mission, not to mention spiritualism and mediumship.

In the Acts of the Apostles, 2 et seq, the author refers to the Pentecost event when a phenomenon like a mighty rushing wind came upon them and tongues like flames of fire dispersed among them and rested upon each one. They were all filled with the Holy Spirit and spoke with tongues.

Anyone can embrace the Holy Spirit, you can actually put your arms around it, it's a column of light. You can photograph it.

Now, that's not blasphemy.

Let me explain why.

In, "Who'd Have Thought It," I try to explain the first time I started with my brother dowsing ley lines, and elsewhere the discovery of the Grail Stone in a cave in Andorra.

As we penetrated further into this mystery, we came to realise that the ley system was governed by number and form.

By number in terms of the number of parallels that exist in the ley line, and by geometrical form in terms of particular function at particular places, the node points of the ley system, stone and tree circles, altars of churches in a good state, private homes where people are spiritually aware, and many other points of focus within the community. In terms of form some three thousand geometrical forms are now known to us, albeit not understood. David Thorpe has coined the word codons to describe these forms

One of the forms we started to encounter was this:

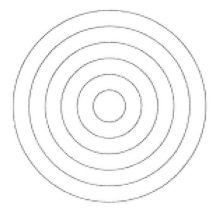

Seven concentric circles

And then, following a form of, seven concentric circles each encased within a square.

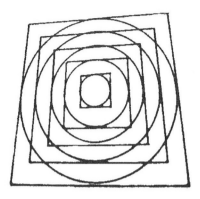

The first form would turn up in what one might call positive situations and the second in what one might call negative.

The seven circles would be found on an altar, around a healer and in other like situations. If you start a healing seminar it manifests within the centre of the group.

It manifests to a dowser as such because he is passing through it and, as it were, taking a cross section, (although I didn't realise that initially).

With the rod, or the hand in place of the rod, if you pass through it you get fourteen reactions. If you walk around each circle, your rod or hand remains closed enabling you to trace the configuration. That's how one determines any geometrical form within the subtle energy system.

When we found that ley lines were ephemeral and not permanent, it was basically the discovery that healers plugged into the ley system, consciously or unconsciously, when they were working that provided the basis for looking at the fields that surrounded them when they were healing. The seven circles become identified with the healer at work.

Later, when working with clairvoyants or people with hypervision, they would say. "There's a column of light on that person." Dowsing it would find the seven circles.

In Spain, when I was working with a lady who had this gift, she described the seven circles as really being seven tubes, one within another, going upwards and each with a different colour, corresponding to the rainbow, or light split up by a prism, except they weren't in the same order. But her explanation and the photographs that emerged from Jesus Castro in his book, "Supervivencia" or "Survival", lead me to believe it was just a segment I was looking at and that it went upwards infinitely. Furthermore, you could embrace it and put your arms around it.

Sig Lonegren, dowser extraordinaire of the USA, refers in his writings to "uppers" and "downers". I believe that what he has perceived as a dowser to be an "upper" is exactly the same thing.

A downer is the reverse. Whereas the "upper" puts positive energy into a situation, the "downer" sucks it out.

I find it present where there has been hatred, violent emotion, lost souls, black magic and the such like. It's a form of black hole you have to seal up and replace with an "upper". It is what some would call an exorcism, but I would call it healing.

All that having been said, "uppers", or if you like, the Holy Spirit, exists within non-Christian cultures. Here's a heresy. Could the Holy Spirit appear in a non-Christian community? Yes.

Healing is not unique to the Christian cultures. It takes place around the whole world. Read Max Freedom Long's books about the Kahuna people in Polynesia. It happens in India in a non-Christian culture.

The poor old Holy Spirit has been looked at in laboratories for the last 150 years by Mesmer, von Reichenbach, Wilhelm Reich and many others.

Mary Coddington sums it all up in her book, "In Search Of The Healing Energy", Excalibur Books, 1981, Northampton. She is referring to von Reichenbach's Odic force as described by Dr Audrey Westlake, whom I once had the honour of meeting on the same platform at the Radionics Conference.

1) Odyle is a universal property of matter in variable and unequal distribution both in space and time.
2) It interpenetrates and fills the structure of the universe. It cannot be isolated or eliminated from anything in nature.
3) It quickly penetrates and courses through everything.
4) It flows in concentrated form from special sources such as heat, friction, sound, electricity, light, the moon, solar and stellar rays, chemical action, organic vital activity of plants and animals, especially man.
5) It possesses polarity. There is both negative odyle, which gives a sensation of coolness, and positive odyle, which gives the sensation of warmth and discomfort.
6) It can be conducted, metals, glass, silk and water being perfect conductors.
7) It is related to a distance, and these rays penetrate through clothes, bedclothes, boards and walls.

8) Substances can be charged with odyle, or odyle may be transferred from one body to another. This is effected by contact, and requires a certain amount of time.

9) It is luminous, either as a luminous glow or as a flame, shinning blue at the negative and yellow red at the positive. These flames can be made to flow in any direction.

10) Human beings are odyle containers with polarity and are luminous over the whole surface, hence the so-called aura surrounding the physical body. In the rhythm, a periodic fluctuation occurs in the human body.

I would like to comment on my own experience in respect of all these propositions:

1) I suspect it to be so but can only regard this as supposition.

2) As Eugene Wigner, I believe it to be so. If not, the universe has no meaning.

3) When you get it going through your consciousness and visualisation, it does run everywhere. It is the universal glue.

4) I agree. Especially man, the repository of consciousness, the divine spark.

5) If it is the same thing as the energy in the ley lines, then it is polar. The two rotating spirals at the heads of the valleys are evidence of this.

6) Yes, it is like that, but even if you consciously drew a circuit on paper, it does the same thing. All things conduct when we wish, above all our own consciousness.

7) As you transmit healing anywhere, even through a Faraday cage, it has to be so.

8) Talismans may be made of anything,

9) It is luminous, at least to me, in the half light, particularly if you have a wooden pendulum over a ley line on a long string. The pendulum glows. It is at the service of visualisation and in the higher consciousness, thus manipulated.

10) Human beings are containers by virtue of their existence and by virtue of their consciousness directors, without this energy we cannot live.

Is the Holy Spirit, Mana, Prana, the ether etc. Is the Holy Spirit the positive or negative part? Is it still? Is the Holy Spirit only the good part? What relationship does it have with consciousness? Is it conscious of itself? Is it the great programme for the evolution of consciousness? Is it a great hologram?

I think it's impossible to know by definition. It remains the Great Mystery. But the list of characteristics given by Mary Coddington is in conformity with my own experience.

But you cannot heal without it, and I believe it to be polar, and it is our choice as to whether it works positively or negatively.

A series of photographs were taken of me at a symposium in Madrid, November 1988 and a comment on this appeared in the Spanish parapsychological magazine Karma-7, in which appeared an interview I had given about healing and in which I referred to the column of light of the Holy Spirit.

At the end of the interview, to my great shock, appeared a following comment.

"When we had finished the article, we were given a photograph of Colin Bloy taken during a speech he had given during the second Symposium on the secret life of Jesus. In the photo, at his side appears a column of light. If we had not been present at the speech, we would have believed it to be a fault in the film but, at the moment it was taken, Mr Bloy was finishing speaking about the energy of the Holy Spirit which he invokes during healing, and which manifests as a great column of white light, and addressing those present had just said, "It's here beside me. Don't you see it?"

We would also like to add that in all the photos in which Colin Bloy appears, the same column of light appears, the same column of light is visible, whereas the photographs of other people in the same conference show no similar phenomenon."

I felt obliged to write the following letter to the Editor:

Dear Sir,

You have kindly published two interviews with myself, about my experiences with the Grail in the Pyrenees and as a spiritual healer, and also speaking of photographs of me where a column of white light of the Holy Spirit appears next to me.

Up to now. Thanks to God, I have never had a reputation for saintliness, nor do I wish to acquire one through a wrong interpretation. Nor do I wish to lose all my friends, nor my beloved other half, Magdalena, who suffers saints not gladly, except on Sundays.

The phenomenon of the Holy Spirit, the column of light, descends on a sincere healer when they are acting with pure love, the love that has no conditions, nor sentimentality, nor hope of reward, save that of fulfilling oneself as a human being. And I know thousands of good healers.

Thus, may I take advantage of this opportunity to say to all my friends in Spain that this is a phenomenon which is available to everyone, and to deny rumours that I am

too many for comfort, now I think about it. Apart from that I'm Anglican and a heretic, as my dear friend Father Jose Maria Marle Pilon, knows very well.

The only member of my family who approaches saintliness is my mother, who is well known for that in many countries, including Spain, and she has frequently travelled with me to ensure that I behave myself, which I have not always done.

I am most grateful for this opportunity to clear up a matter which could have spoiled my life, although it is true that I do pray to God every day to make good, but not yet!

Your Sincerely

Well, I hope that clarifies my feelings that sanctimoniousness serves no purpose in this business.

Yes, that's the way it works, bit it's there for all of us, not just me.

Chapter 40

Healing Animals

Animals may be healed in the same way as human beings.

Their energy bodies, however, are different.

I've had this argument before with certain ladies, and have retired with a bloody nose, but animals do not, as far as I can see and feel, have chakras in the sense that human beings do.

I cannot find or call any similar configuration, nor can I find more than half the genetic coding of humans. These are inflammatory statements, I know, and many umbrellas will be laid on my head, but there you are.

However, various cases of infection in dogs seem to have been cured.

One day in November 1988 Magdalena phoned me. "The vet is here," she said, "One of the Dobermanns has an infection which she says is very serious and can affect human beings. She has haemorrhages in the nose. The vet wants to put her down. Otherwise she needs a course of anti-biotics and careful nursing for several months in a dog's hospital, because the children are at risk. What shall I do?"

I talked to the vet and she told me the same thing.

"Do you want me to heal her?" I asked Magdalena.

"Go on, then," she said.

"Send her to me," I replied, somewhat doubting because I wanted no risk to the children.

At distance, I felt the dog, and asked for the archetype of the virus.

The name was leichmamiosis.

I talked to it just as I had to Magdalen's impetigo.

A week later she told me the dog was well, and had no traces of the condition, confirmed by a somewhat surprised vet.

About the same time, my mother phoned to say that an Alsatian that belonged to her friend Joan also had serious haemorrhages in the nose.

At a distance, I called the dog and removed the polyp or lump that was causing the problem with an etheric operation, within two days the condition disappeared.

The conclusion of this is that humans can heal animals.

Later, Joan's other dog had a large growth on its eyelid. Following an etheric operation at a distance, it disappeared within days.

My mother's neighbour's dogs were treated and showed great improvement in what was basically old age.

Chapter 41

Drug Addiction and Healing

At various times, but without taking the matter further, I had noticed that people who had been smoking marijuana seemed to have lost all their vital energy.

One day in February, a Tarot reader Magdalena and I knew in Spain came to ask if I would look at a friend of hers, a man of some 30 years who was addicted to heroin, and was going cold turkey.

Looking at him, there was clearly no vital energy, the chakras were in chaos, the five essential archetypal forms were in a similar state, the assemblage point, pointing downwards, and the karmic lattice virtually unrecognisable. Also, the genetic code was messy

I put these right and waited to see the effect.

Twenty-four hours later his fields were surprisingly good, and he said he felt he had more energy. It occurred to me to ask for the archetypal form of heroin addiction, and I was given the following:

Two amorphous spheres, and I invited it to leave.

I then asked if there was an "aversion" therapy and was given a perfect circle of the basic human archetype. I had restored that at the first session. It seems logical. Restoring one's basic integrity would remove any dependency, if it can be maintained.

During a visit to Barcelona in March 1991, the suggestion was made that we visit a drug rehabilitation clinic near Villfranca del Penedes, several hours drive out of Barcelona.

The centre is basically an old farmhouse with about a dozen young people in rehabilitation. It is run by a very dedicated couple on a voluntary basis. There is some financial help from the local authority but not much.

The programme is very much orientated to the outdoor life, healthy eating, hard work and physical exercise. They seem to be quite successful.

I had had little experience, if any in such matters but it was thought I could help with healing. At least, I felt that I could do something to help.

I was impressed by the good, healthy and loving atmosphere. There was nothing negative there either in inmates or directors twelve unfortunates were lined up before me and I sought to put them at their ease at being confronted by the unlikely circumstances of being analysed and healed by an Englishman who arrived out of no-where. Fortunately, I got them laughing quickly and it was possible in such a sample to draw some conclusions.

1) Nine had no energy in the first energy body.
2) None had enough.

3) Ten had complications in the archetypes of their essential fields.
4) All had good harmony in the chakras.
5) The general health was good.
6) The assemblage point cord of ten was at the lowest point.
7) All had disturbances in the archetypal labyrinths of their consciousness.

Mabel and I put right what we had perceived to be wrong and it remains to be seen what will emerge.

In any event, one may conclude that a very significant effect of drug intoxication is at the interface of spirit consciousness and perception. If these may be assisted to return to normal, it might be crucial in the whole matter and provide as basis for their trying to rid themselves of drugs and to have much more control over themselves from the spirit and thus find it easier to make a complete recovery.

I heard from Brunni, some weeks later, that the husband had phoned to say that there had been a most significant improvement across the board.

I hope we have learned something important which healers everywhere may use to help this "incubus" on our contemporary society.

Chapter 42

The Channels Of Command Of The Brain

After having worked on the archetypes of consciousness, the labyrinth, it occurred to us, taking the analogue further, that we might be able to look at the brain function in terms of giving instructions to the body, in a similar way, and having asked for the appropriate form, this was given.

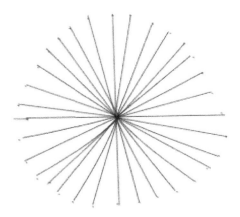

A series of 32 radii from a central point. Now at the time of writing, I have no idea what the attributions one might give to each channel, bit someone suffering from Parkinson's did exhibit a foreshortening of numbers 19, 20 and 21, but it is a bit early to see the effect it has, but I include it as a bit of latest news which maybe important in various illnesses of a motor nature.

Chapter 43

Genetic Code & Archetypal Forms

The ideal form appears as 4 ovals with 16 points on the edge of the ovals. Differing conditions show themselves with certain points missing on one of the four ovals.

Forms of Infection

Common Cold

Gonorrhoea

Syphilis

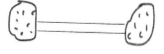

Mumps

Cancer

Impetigo

Flu

Salmonella

Measles

German Measles

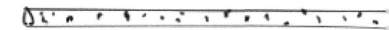

Chicken Pox

And so on. You can find others yourself.

Forms of Blood

After some experience with archetypal forms, it occurred to us to look at the blood and see if it had an available archetypal form. Eight lozenges in a row, long side to long side, all equal in size and smooth.

The only thing that I understand about it so far is that each section refers to an aspect and putting it right when it was missing or chaotic, helps. I believe one for instance, as to do with trace elements, but it is only a beginning.

The Immune System

The immune system looks like a string of pearls. As yet I cannot define potential aspects, but again, putting things right when they are chaotic, seems to help.

The Endocrine System

The endocrine system looks like, eight forms like flowers in a line, each with eight petals. I am sure that each one refers to a different gland.

The Hormonal System

Work still needs to be done on this system. But at present it is showing itself as four ovals, (as a string necklace,) with 6 bands around each oval. Is each oval a different hormone?

The Nervous System

The nervous system is as follows. I have no idea where to begin with this and yet to find someone with a noticeable change from the archetype.

Organs

It also occurred that maybe an even quicker check of an organ could be achieved through its archetypal form if it had one. I asked for the heart and to my surprise it was:

I have since found someone suffering from angina and the form was:

The lungs are this:

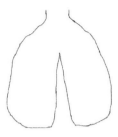

People with lung cancer seem to have excrescences on the inner edge of the archetype. It is too early to say whether they are helpful in healing or merely diagnostic.

The stomach is this:

The liver:

The kidneys left and right:

The intestines:

These may be put into a whole schematic as follows.

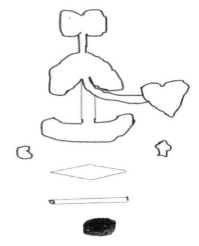

I include a circle at the very end to cover the smaller organs both male and female. If not complete, it indicates that further investigation is necessary. The minor organs may be examined by associating a circle to each one, ie gall bladder, but in female organs experience has recently shown that the following are forms of:

1) Fallopian tube

2) Womb

The above may be read as a schematic with the fingers in about 10 seconds with practice.

Blood Pressure

In seeking to establish whether there was an archetypal route to determining whether an individual generally had high or low blood pressure the form that emerged was as follows.

Normal

And it is as if a little arrow on one side indicates the result. It is be presumed that projecting it to normal helps the problem.

Skin Archetype

In Barcelona, Angel told me that since the last course he attended, he had established that when healing skin complaints he had looked for the archetypal form and found the following.

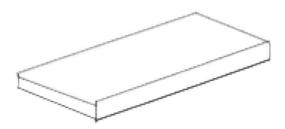

Where there were problems, this would appear irregular, wrinkled or spotty. Returning it to its standard form was helpful.

A lot of work needs to be done here as well.

Chapter 44

Platonic Solids

A further dimension to it all is added by the function of the Divine Proportion, whose symbol is a circle with a vertical line through the centre. In the egg there is an evolution of the Platonic Solids that may be observed. In conversations with David Wood, the author of "Genesis", he made the point that the platonic solids are based on this symbol, that they can only evolve to five, before returning to the beginning, which set me thinking. Also, in their book "Occult Chemistry," Leadbetter and Besant talk about etheric atoms being behind physical atoms, and make the statement that the etheric atoms are formed by combinations of the Platonic Solids.

David also made the point that the above Divine Proportion symbol governs forms of the new chakras as well, the sunflower, the polyhedron, the wings, the egg, the spiral, etc. It might be extremely important. The circle with a line going through the apex and the nadir vertically, symbol might be the essential governing principle of material manifestation.

Chapter 45

Matchstick Man

It was at a Barcelona seminar whilst we were running through the archetypal organ forms, that it occurred to me we could possibly make an even quicker initial check of an individual. Thus, the matchstick man or woman came into being.

If someone had a spinal problem the matchstick man appeared like this.

A heart problem would be:

One could therefore take a very quick initial view of the part of the physical body that was affected.

One of the things we were learning at the same time was that although it was now possible for an experienced person to do a complete analysis in perhaps 30 seconds. It was nonetheless true that it is important to spend time with the person in front of you and never overlook the power of suggestion.

Many of the cynics have said of spiritual and faith healers. "Of course, it is all suggestion."

What an interesting observation.

In the first instance, to gain the confidence of the person needing healing is an objective that scarcely needs stating. Of course, it is important. Elsewhere I have sought to show there are many ways of healing, even fear as in the army or by the advent of Christmas.

But if there is a genuine recognition of the power of suggestion in healing by the positivist lobby, why don't they make more of a study of it and seek to find out how to provoke it deliberately.

The answer is that if you approach suggestion in a positivist way, you lose it. If you say to someone, "Look I am going to suggest to you that you get better," that has only a limited efficacy.

I have no doubt that to relax somebody into a dream-like state and entrain their psyche into co-operation with their own improvement works. Particularly with skin complaints and various conditions which admit of a positivist diagnosis.

I remember Carmen in Salamanca who suffered from a very strange scale like skin condition who showed a very dramatic improvement after two or three sessions. Perhaps deeper hypnosis can achieve more dramatic effects, but that is an area with which I have not felt comfortable.

As a consequence of the Matchstick man, it helps us to get more quickly to the point, but gives us more time to communicate on a simple human level.

An experienced was gained with the use of the archetypal or schematic forms, more evidence was manifested of the subtle causes or some illnesses. It was at a weekend seminar in the new Healing Centre, in Madrid that we learned more about the diagnosis of illness. When we are going through the check list no attempts at correction were made until the very end. Then we would work through the check list to see if, for instance, when a karmic correction was made, other deficient features, such as the genetic code, were corrected. It was so in some cases. Correcting the genetic code automatically corrected other features, such as the nervous system.

This we developed the discipline of check first and correct afterwards.

It was increasingly satisfying that the majority of those attending the seminars had no difficulty in identifying the archetype with their hands.

CAUTION Matchstick man can only be considered as an initial rudimentary check. It should not be relied on but merely used as a pointer to areas requiring more profound analysis.

Chapter 46

The Labyrinths of Consciousness

The sequence of forms that came from the Andorran stone ended in a series of labyrinths. Here are the last two.

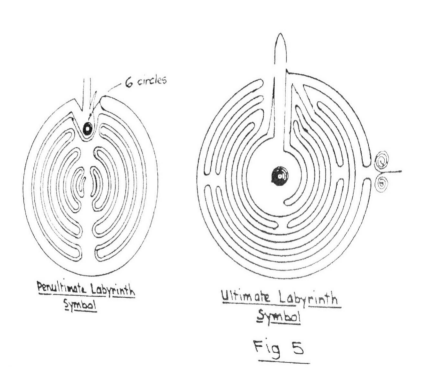

Penultimate Labyrinth Symbol

Ultimate Labyrinth Symbol

Fig 5

Some-time after this experience, we went to visit Trevor Ravenscroft at his London home. Trevor sadly no longer in our dimension, was the author of that remarkable book, "The Spear of Destiny." The object of our visit was to consult him over the whole Grail Stone affair.

I shall always remember the moment when he said, "Of course you found the proletarian Grail," which was some comfort.

It should be said that Trevor's views on spiritual realities were very much formed by Walter Johannes Stein, an intimate of Rudolph Steiner, and author of some remarkable books, including "World History in the Light of the Holy Grail – Ninth Century" in 1928, and also Gunter Wachsmuth, who wrote a book in the same period called "Etheric Formative Forces in Cosmos, Nature and Man, in which may be found explanations which make much sense of the Andorra experience. Trevor was a real anthroposophist, and helped my understanding of what had happened most considerably.

I pointed out to him on one of the frequent occasions when we subsequently met, the various labyrinth shapes that formed the final part of the sequence of geometrical forms.

"Of course," he said, "They are representations of the human man," looking at the final two as illustrated earlier.

There is a penultimate you have what you would call Piscean consciousness. The left and right hemispheres are separate and the concentric circles, which represent the pineal gland's contact with the cosmic intelligence are isolated from both.

I looked at the last with more understanding and continued the analogy. In this figure, then, the two hemispheres had intertwined, the concentric circles, were now contained within it, but the two new features were the Gothic arch formation protruding in front, and the ram's horn spiral to the right rear.

When the form appeared in the garden in Andorra when I first detected this line, it was interesting to recall that the ram's horn spirals had formed a line that went down the valley. I followed this line and had found at the end of it in the undergrowth a small stone circle.

I also recalled the extraordinary photo of the lady who had the visions at San Damiano in Italy, and how in spite of the obvious flaring of higher consciousness in the crown chakra, and how the dragon energy of the earth formed part of her being, manifesting as a dark brown energy at her feet. Maybe the lesson was that in our corporeal state, we should never neglect the dragon basic vitality.

What then might be the meaning of the projecting form of the Gothic arch at what one should suppose to be the forehead? A reasonable explanation might be based on the alchemical principle, which requires the refinement of the spirit so that it is able to influence the material world. Thus, the combined effect of the higher consciousness and the energy of the dragon may manifest in physical change as say, in healing.

Over the years, I have noticed that those who had developed spiritually, and used it as healers or channels manifested a horn from their brow as an energy field. Indeed, I began to feel that the reason that that mythical beast, the unicorn, was used as a symbol for esoteric knowledge was as a result of this phenomenon. And with further experience, I noted that the horn in fact was more like a three-dimensional Gothic arch than a conventional horn.

I then formulated the concept that the last labyrinth could be held to represent the Grail consciousness of the Aquarian Age, and as I write this in 1991, I note that it is the year of the Maze, and that a book called "The Art of the Maze" has been published, written by Adrian Fisher and that a Museum of Mazes is to open in Herefordshire.

All the aforementioned, hopefully has its own internal logic, given the correct observation of the two labyrinth forms and the objective nature of the Andorran phenomenon.

But that having been said, was the phenomenon a way of explaining something, or had it a more functional significance?

This had all occurred some years before the contacts with Carl Jung and Hassim, and the growing awareness of the objective nature of Jung's concept of archetypal forms in the collective consciousness, and the application of the principle to healing, as I have sought to explain earlier, in that remarkable productive weekend healing seminar in Madrid, which appeared to open new understanding of the higher chakras, and the energies present in some way were increasing the group perceptions, we were looking a distance at someone's brain, where there were problems. In the examination the idea started to develop that, whereas we had been looking at an archetypal form which had a mushroom shape and could be held to represent the physical brain, was it possible to establish the relationship between the organ and the state of consciousness? So, thinking, an imperfect simple maze form appeared between my hands and set off a whole new investigation and reassessment of the essential nature of the labyrinth as an archetype,

The proposition that the labyrinth is a primordial form is not unreasonable and surfaces in petroglyphs and art forms in many parts of the world and in many epochs – it is not really necessary to elaborate further. I now assume therefore, that in its purest manifestation it represents an archetypal statement about the nature of consciousness.

Whereas the ladder of consciousness may be seen to manifest in the chakras, culminating in the sixteenth chakra of the Grail cup, as we have discussed earlier.

One Saturday morning in February 1990, I sat down and asked if there was a labyrinth form which corresponded to each chakra, and if so, what were they?

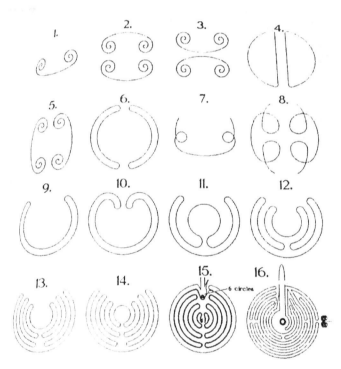

The Labyrinthine Forms associated with the first Sixteen Chakras

Of course, the labyrinths have close connections with the series of forms that emerged from the Andorran Stone, and it can be argues that there is a significant element of my own subjective perceptions here.

The first thing to notice is that there is a reasonably coherent evolution from the first figure, the double dragon spiral, to the labyrinth of the Grail consciousness in the sixteenth chakra. There may be a significant relationship between these figures, and the Hindu concept of Kundalini, the coiling double dragon energy that stimulates consciousness as it rises through the spine or chakras of the ladder of consciousness.

If the use of archetypal forms in the healing of the physical body is analogous, then the improvement of consciousness through the same technique appears possible.

I remember the case of a youth who died of hydro encephalitis – water on the brain – and the post mortem revealed that 90% of the brain cavity was simply liquid. The coroner in his wisdom saw fit to commiserate with the parents for having had to care for a vegetable. The parents vigorously repudiated this, saying that his mental functions had been perfectly normal until his death. Thus, one may separate out the organ of the brain from consciousness, and to that extent, it may be available to healers to help brain damaged people to have improved consciousness by working through the labyrinths.

It should become another routine check for the healer to ascertain that the first eight chakras are exhibiting the correct archetypal form of consciousness in the area of the brain. It really does help and there is a lot more to learn.

Assisting the individual to rise in consciousness is significant, if not the most significant aspect of spiritual healing. It later occurred to me that it might be possible to determine the average level of consciousness of individuals, and asked for the archetypal form which might indicate that, a sixteen bar ladder appeared in my hands, and in running the fingers simultaneously up either side, according to particular individual, a gap would indicate the answer, thus one might conclude that an individual might be a predominantly base, heart or crown chakra person, and to the extent that a raising of consciousness of that individual the raising of the point on the archetypal scale could be achieved through visualisation and projection.

It may be very helpful in stimulating the individual to participate in their own healing, as the presumption I make is that the higher consciousness, the easier and clearer are the visualisations of one's own improvement.

Returning some eight weeks later to the drug rehabilitation centre, we found that there was two who had not been present at the first meeting. There was a discernible difference in their demeanour and in their eyes. We treated them in the same way.

The directors, Martin and Josefina expressed themselves very positively in favour of healing and asked us to return again.

Chapter 47

A Mutation in Human Consciousness

In April this year I met Shauna Crocket, dear Shauna in Madrid. Yes, her plane was late, but there you are. That is Shauna. Shauna is a remarkable lady and "Link-up" is one illustrious monument to her work so far. She once saved Fountain. But she is always late.

As we talked, she said, "Do you know there's an etheric change in DNA?"

Her question crystallised many things that I and others, as healers and dowsers, had been observing over the last ten years and particularly after the Harmonic Convergence.

Dowsing had seen the 7 factor in the ley lines move to 8 in 1978, and after Harmonic Convergence move to a 16 factor, or a double 8.

It was shortly to be noticed that we were able to look at more energy bodies than the first, in what has been called the etheric, and the second that people seem to call the astral.

Jacques Deriu, who has been a reliable forecaster in these matters, said that there were now 16 energy bodies available for analysis, but we were likely to understand more than the first six in my lifetime.

What he then said, shortly after Harmonic Convergence, set me and others looking for more chakras than the traditional 7, and in the first edition of this book. I tried to make the first report about the new, or recently accessible chakras, with the Cup of the Grail in 16th position.

Friends in Madrid in the Fountain Group there have contributed to a greater understanding of these chakras.

Now the number 8 seems important in all this. If the Age of Pisces were governed by the 7, the number 8 considered to be the number of spiritual regeneration manifested in Gothic architecture of the Templars, and more particularly in fonts and pulpits, which produce a particular energy.

Now current thinking suggests that there is a fundamental mutation in human consciousness. Alexander Neklessa, of the Synla Institute in Moscow, has talked to Fountain about this. So, when Shauna made her point, I thought about the work we had been doing in looking at the archetypal or etheric form of the genetic code. It looked like four ellipses, strung together like beads, and eight points on either side of each ellipse.

Now over the last few years, we had noticed that instead of the classic 64 of the DNA, we were seeing in children born in those years 10 points per side rather than 8.

It was as if there was indeed some form of mutation at least of consciousness. Dolores, a dear hospital Matron in Madrid, explained to me that she (and she is a few months away from retirement), had noticed in the last few years that babies were different. They were born with their eyes open. They had hair. They looked at you immediately in a questioning way. Something was happening.

I also remember some friends who said to me that they had recently done a course on immortality and would I look at their genetic code? It was based on a 10, which was different at any rate. Now I am not sure what their courses involved, nor am I particularly in favour of immortality – I am in favour of heightened perception an abandonment of the left hemisphere of the brain as the only means of perceiving reality.

Perhaps that is what it is all about.

Clive Wood, and Oxford medical biologist, recently confirmed to me that the DNA is kept in repair. "By what?" I asked. "Aha," he said.

We seemed to agree that there must be a master plan behind the DNA – Goethe's "Urpflanze"?

At any rate, with Santigo and Rosabel in Madrid having been through the chakras together, they responded to my question - given that 10's were being born now as opposed to the traditional 8's to have the shift to the 10 made for them by a healer? Their answer was yes, it was possible.

As I sat talking to Shauna in Madrid, and said. "What am I?"

An 8," I replied. "Do you want to be a 10?"

"I'll ask permission," she said.

After a few moments she said, "I have permission."

I did it, through visualisation. So, let us see what happens and what Shauna's testimony will be.

It maybe we have put our finger on a crucial point for the future of humanity, On the other hand we may be talking arrant nonsense. It is worth finding out.

I have to say as a postscript that there is preliminary evidence that those who were born 8's can actually become 10's through self-knowledge and self-development.

It is very preliminary, but it is only fair after Shauna's perceptive review of this book that she could be the subject of such an experiment, particularly as it may never have been necessary.

Chapter 48

The Fourth Energy Body

At a session in Barcelona with Maria-Asunta, Angel and others, we thought we might look at the fourth energy body.

We all looked together as if it were as an archetypal form and decided that it had one rather like corrugated paper.

We took this to be the ideal form.

What did it mean? What variations might it have? We tried to look at that aspect and found that it opened up like a flower.

Or like a banana skin, said someone. What does it mean? Perhaps it is a lotus. Something like that? It seems like an opening, as if the person were liberating himself or herself. It is like a butterfly emerging from the pupa, as if the person is going through a threshold of perception.

It may be so. As yet it remains to be rationalised. How does it fit in with the chakras, the ladder of consciousness, with the angle of the cord?

The question is raised, what is perception? The perception of the 5 senses is a given. We may be aware of subtle perceptions, new forms of consciousness. Whither mediumship, clairvoyance.

We have spoken at length about Gurdjieff's courses of waking up. How this may lead to self-awareness, to Valery's third state of awareness. The word consciousness has been used frequently as a generic term relating to perception. If this is a line of enquiry is pointed in the right direction perhaps the question can be posed as to whether consciousness in its higher state opens the doors to various forms of perception and what those forms might be?

During August 1990, Sixto Paz Wells, a Peruvian contactee who had been "up there", some five times, came to England to tell his story. He and friends came to see me as I knew him from meetings in Spain. I did some interpreting for him and on checking his energy bodies noticed how his fourth energy body was clearly peeled back as a banana, which gives further impetus to the theory that the fourth is a perception barrier. His angelic wings of the twelfth chakra were clearly open.

In his story he does say that was he to attended "up there" to help develop himself.

I hasten to say that the message he brought back is essentially to get on with "Fountain type" work, which is why it was always comfortable to work with him.

Over to you.

Chapter 49

Some Thoughts On The Objectivity of Archetypes

I accept that the Marian appearances. Indeed, I frequently visit a site near Escorial monastery in Spain, where 20,000 people may gather on the first Saturday of the month. I have spoken with several who have seen her, simple people, academics, engineers, none of them have any doubts. I have a photo taken by a friend of an appearance. She takes the classic form of religious icons. Many photos taken there have strange effects. I have seen just such a collection and they are most impressive. The whole area, where there is a healing spring, has a grove of willow trees, great granite rocks and a Druidic air about it. Air natural temple of natural religion.

I am nonetheless struck by the fact that Mary appears to Christian communities and is easily recognised, the Lourdes statue is in the classic form. If you dowse the area of Escorial and around the tree of the first appearance, the concentric circles of the column of light are there. I am sure that what night be called the feminine principle of the earth does manifest, in an archetypal form.

The question is, does the archetype depend on the observer for its apparent form or upon the phenomenon itself?

I find Carl Jung's views on UFO's persuasive. A technological society can perceive certain phenomena as nuts and bolts spaceships. A non-technological society will see something else.

As Ezekiel saw a fiery chariot, that was his perception. I feel that subtle beings and energies tend to be perceived in terms of the vocabulary of the imagery and concepts of the observer. Thus "Mary" may appear as the female goddess to another community conditioned to a different vocabulary. It does not invalidate the phenomena.

So, it may be with the dowsing of the archetypes to healing, not to mention the cup of the 16th chakra. As Emma Louise von Frany – Jung's daughter in law has said. "The image of the cup or Grail is the most potent myth of humanity.

By looking for its form, perhaps we were drawn to interpret it in that form for that reason. After all, it is a bit odd that a chakra should take the form of a human artefact. But if we are looking at the highest available form of consciousness. It would be the form that represents that to our subconscious minds and thus the energy is dowsed in that form.

It may be so with the other archetypes of the heart, lungs etc. They appear even child- like, viz matchstick man and so on. That they are shared intellectual artefacts is most likely, but they represent the easiest way to perceive an archetype or derivations. The most important thing of all is that it works. But they are at the interface of the subjective and the objective.

Conclusion

It has not been easy to write this book. But I offer it as a sharing, rather than a self- advertisement. I hope the day will come sooner rather than later, when a healer is no longer a special person. It should be part and parcel of one's daily relations with one's neighbour.

How, therefore, do I cope with my own ego? Simply as follows, you can do what I do. The more of you who do it, the less important will I and my fellows be, and the fewer ego problems we will have. In a sense, it's up to you, not us, it's a sharing.

Healers today have the obligation to prevent illness, at all levels, illness being a departure from harmony, indirect or direct. They should seek to work with orthodox medicine, not reject it, though orthodox medicine must also change its model and work with healers. Healers should avoid miracles unless they are necessary, make old age easy and death sweet, and seek always to share such knowledge as they have with others, so that they are never a race set apart. They should enjoy a simple attitude of mind which all beings can share and apply to their neighbour to the extent that being a healer is without comment. We are all healers. We can all go down to the pub and do a few miracles.

Healing is not an art or technology. It is an attitude of mind towards one's neighbour and the cosmos. It is a spiritual science. Those who heal are aware. They must share their awareness with others. Healing does not extend uniquely to individuals. It extends to communities and to the world and the cosmos. It's about self-awareness and self-identification with the whole.

The whole is hologrammatic, and consciousness, i.e. self awareness, is the stuff of the universe. There are archetypes, ideas, coefficients, contrasts, variables, but all of this only has meaning if humanity can wake itself up, acknowledge the third state of awareness, live in it more often than not so creation with God, the original idea, becomes possible. That's what creation was really all about.

Healing of individuals works, hence healing of the planet works. The planet is a being. We are all cells within it, just as one member of a team.

Newtonian physics created the technology that sent a human being to the Moon, but we are still sitting in the corner of the Cosmos, the manifestation of pure consciousness. Healing our neighbour is one thing, healing the planet is another. Pursing spiritual science so that corporeal man triumphs in the spirit and assumes his wider responsibilities is yet another. Do not get the idea that to be spiritually aware is wimpish. It's pretty demanding, but when you learn to love with conditions as a way of life, then it all works.

GO FOR IT. It is our divine heritage as God's creatures.

WAKE UP! IT'S ALL THERE IF YOU REALLY WANT IT!

In one word

LOVE

Appendix 1

Healing Check List

1. Look At The Sick Person.
   This can tell you a lot through simple experience and common sense.
2. Check Basic Energy.
   This may be done by running the hands around the trunk of the body. Where someone is ill and has not had healing, there is frequently no perceptible energy. Thus, in order even to detect weaknesses of the energy field, the administering of basic energy is a pre-condition.
3. Check New Field For Weak Points.
   This will tell you where problems exist. Check extremities, arms and legs to establish if the field is uniform. Where it attenuates in the limbs, there is usually a problem, actual or potential, of circulation, rheumatism, arthritis, etc. There may be specific points that can only be detected with the finger-tip.
4. Check Spine For Free Energy Flow.
   This is best done with the finger-tip. In some cases the spine may have no energy at all, and correcting it in itself produces a general improvement in the person. Where there are individual points with no energy, the person will probably be complaining of problems there. Using the pointing finger and the visualisation technique is the way to get this right.
5. Check Individual Organs And Main Nerve Canals.

Run your hand in a more concentrated way around the individual's body, thinking of heart, lungs, kidneys etc., one by one. A healer doesn't have to be an expert in anatomy necessarily. With the fingertips nerve canals may be checked. The important thing is to know where healing energy is required. Decide whether etheric operation is necessary. If so, and you can, do it.

6. Check Chakras.

Switching the mode to chakras rather than etheric energy, the spiritual, mental, psychic and emotional states may be determined quickly. Keeping these in balance is a vital part of healing. Depressed people don't get well quickly, or people whose emotions are bruised and battered, thus some opening of the crown chakra is very important.

Psychism which is not understood can confuse and bewilder. A quick way to balance the chakras is to visualise, in any size necessary for convenience, the following figure of 8 ellipses (in a row on top of each other,) which represents the eight chakras, and give it back to the person. The extension of the crown or heart chakra can be established where necessary.

7. Check Archetype And Dependent Forms, And Infections

Call them one by one and put them right where necessary. Call negativity and compress it, where it exists, into a cube, sending any excess to the Source with love. Check for archetypes of any germ, virus and cancer.

8. Check Assemblage Point

If less than 45 degrees, make it so. It helps perception improvements in consciousness allow the individuals to participate more in their own healing.

243

9. Check Karma

   Where there is not a perfect ladder of 32 rungs, make it right.

10. Check Second and Third Energy Bodies

    Where there are irregularities or "visitors", make good and send "intruders" back to the Source gently.

11. AT ALL TIMES REMAIN CHEERFUL, CONFIDENT – WITHOUT BEING RIDICULOUS, MAINTAIN EYE CONTACT, TOUCH THE PERSON TO CREATE GREATER CONFIDENCE.

12. LOVE THAT PERSON WITH ALL YOUR SOUL, AND DESIRE THEIR HEALING, NEVER FORGET THE HEALER'S INSURANCE POLICY WHEN YOU FEEL IN DIFFICULTIES – "PLEASE HELP ME GOD."

Another aspect of illness that healers would do well to look at is the family environment. Many times in Salamanca, parents have brought their children and it should be a matter of routine to check the parents as well. Very often, parents who are low in energy, or suffering from some potential illness, unconsciously take energy from their children, or the children who subconsciously need energy from their parents, don't have a source near them.

Certain illnesses, therefore, may have a collective solution, as well as cause.

Appendix 2

Andorran Meditation

The Earth is a being. It is sick. Heal it in the same way that you would heal an individual. Community healing is the business of Fountain International. When it is truly international, then all the races may heal the planet and all its members and the Kingdoms.

This meditation may last for half an hour. Those who take part should be completely sure they are ready for it. Do not take this meditation lightly.

General Relaxation

1) Visualise a golden hemisphere of light covering the group, and through the centre of this golden hemisphere, see a column of light descend into the middle of the gathering. Set aside daily consciousness, and come together as a group within higher consciousness, to form one being of pure love. The ego is of no significance.

2) The group being starts to identify with the whole of the planet. Starting at the very centre of the earth, in the mega heat and working slowly outwards in a great spiral, being one with the magma – then the hardening rock – issuing slowly at the surface – becoming one with the mineral world in all its elements. Uniting with the dragon energy of the earth, through all its mountains, valleys, fault lines, plains, rivers, seas, then out into

space to the outer edges of the invisible fields that are part of the planet.

3) Identify with the biological earth – the humus – organic life – primitive organisms – lichens – emergent plants – savannahs, grass, cereals, flowers, herbs, fruit trees, the great forests – and the whole process of life within the plant kingdom. Bring the dragon energy into it with love, gentleness and the authority pf pure unselfish consciousness.

4) Now to the animal kingdom. The life giving energies of the dragon now combined with the plant kingdom give rise to primitive life forms, which in turn evolve into the insect kingdoms, and the whole of animal life – pulsing in harmony with the basic energies of the planet, The dragon lives in the animal world in harmony.

5) Back in time, to the various epochs, some millennium away, when emerging consciousness took the form of man. Through fits and starts, and external interventions, see evolution of man being of higher consciousness, moments of harmony, moments of discord, confused at times, clear at others, struggling with his environment – uncertain, at times lonely and desperate, at times illuminated and harmonious – ever struggling to make sense of his adventure on this planet.

6) See recorded history. The struggles for domination by one group over another. The emergence of the idea of love and its shattering as its fragility breaks each time it is put to the test.

7) See the emergence of tribes and nations, with all their pride, arrogance, glories and disasters. The many races, at times seeking to destroy each other and reaching a harmonious accommodation – then falling again.

8) See the occasional teacher who seeks to show the way in love and light – the occasional beacon that shines as one great messenger, speaks for a brief moment and fades. How his message is sometimes incorporated in a state of institution to have a longer but emptier life, and is perverted into a cause for bloodshed.

9) See how more recent teachers represent the true understanding of love – whatever their cultural or ethnic circumstance – and see how some pervert the knowledge for personal gain, and how man slowly and painfully grows in consciousness and awareness, but fails for lack of faith, to practice love in their daily lives, and develops instead the arrogance of reason, and a man centred universe, which can be organised according to the will of the most powerful human groups. The rise of science and technology, harnessed for state and political reasons to create domination for one group or another – and that the pursuit of reason alone has now brought man's adventure on this planet to the edge of total disaster.

10) See how man's increasing penetration into the moving forces of life and the cosmos is eventually showing that the materialist explanation is becoming increasingly unsatisfactory, and that the sciences of man are beginning to realise that what they are looking at is – HOW GOD WORKS – and that the missing part of all the equations is Consciousness – which is an objective field. And that the highest form of THE PURE, UNSENTIMENTAL, UNCONDITIONAL IDENTIFICATION WITH THE EVOLUTION OF TOTAL CONSCIOUSNESS FOR THE WHOLE – LOVE

11) Go forward in time to a period when Gaia finally as a harmonious, complete, loving planet, in which all its members

have evolved sufficiently to return to group consciousness in a totally and understanding act. When the whole human race acts as one with itself and its component parts as a deliberate way if life, and in harmony with the rest of the cosmos.

12) Now take the archetype of the perfection of man – the androgyne – the sum total of male and female – of dragon and cosmos – of yin and yang – complete and integrated – trembling on the brink of his cosmic destiny.

13) Holding that model. Return to the present day and see man currently as he is. Now consider the labyrinth in history as myth, and in practice, as it appears in diagrams in many civilizations. The magnetic fields of the earth are like the labyrinth, which is the representation of the human brain, left and right hemisphere separated, See the new labyrinth developing in which the separate parts start to integrate, to become the total integrated structure that may best seen at Chartes Cathedral. See the coming together of rational man with intuitive man – see physical knowledge finally merge with spiritual knowledge.

14) Understand Golgotha, the place of the skull, and the crisis of consciousness that took place there and similar places in other cultures of man. Understand the message of Osiris, and the bringing together again all the separate parts of man. Understand the light of the East and the message of the Buddha. Understand the real truth of Mohammed. Understand the message of Quetzalcoatl and the unity amongst all races.

15) Now see the planet as energy, for ultimate energy is consciousness. Take the archetype of man and the whole planet into your consciousness as one inseparable energy being. See the dragons of East and West, North and South cease their vortical movement and fuse into the straight lines of man's

consciousness. See the links between villages strengthen, between villages and towns, between towns and cities, between cities and whole nations, between nation and nation, continent and continent. See al frontiers fall, and all divisions disappear. See the body of man and the planet. One whole vibrant being, in joy and harmony, with all its meridians and energy points functioning.

16) And now, go through the complete being, as you would go through an individual when you are healing, and clean it completely.

Take a clean blue light from above and use it as a broom which sweeps before it all man's collective diseases – better known as the seven deadly sins.

Take them one by one

Pride

Jealousy

Hatred

Greed

And so on.

The most dangerous of all is Pride of Spirit, that some how we are better than others because of doing this.

This must be done with total humility.

Sweep out all these lurking demons and archetypes from the being Gaia, and its inseparable inhabitant man: expelled once and for all from our misery ridden existence to the farthest and most distant corners of the universe, never again to trouble man.

See the great being, the archetypal consciousness of the whole universe in majesty, binding again all negative influences to his will, and bring them back to whole again.

Leviathan Bound

And know that in LOVE, man can henceforth participate consciously in his evolution on this planet.

Holding the image of man in perfection in harmony with the planet, healed of his diseases.

Come very slowly back, breath slowly, take a lot of time, don't talk. Relax very, very slowly, and when you really feel that you are back, give thanks to the Source, and embrace your neighbour.

Appendix 3

Proclamation of the
Church of Love

It has no fabric – only understanding.

It has no membership – save those who know they can belong.

It has no rivals – because it is non-competitive.

It has no ambition because it only seeks to serve.

It knows of no boundaries, for nationalism is unloving.

It is not of itself because it seeks to enrich all groups and religions.

It acknowledges all great teachers of all the ages who have shown the truth of love.

Those who participate, practice the truth of love in all their daily being.

There is no walk of life or nationality that is a barrier.

Those who are, know.

It seeks not to teach but to be, and by being, enrich.

It recognizes the collectivity of all humanity and that we are all one with the one.

It recognizes that the way we are may be the way of those around us because we are that way.

It recognizes the whole planet as a being, of which we are part.

It recognizes that the time has come for the supreme transmutation, the ultimate alchemical act, the conscious change of the ego into a voluntary return to the whole.

It does not proclaim itself in a loud voice but in the subtle realms of loving.

It salutes all those in the past who blazoned the path but paid the price.

It admits of no hierarchy or structure, for no one is greater than another.

Its members shall know each other by their deeds and being and their eyes and by no other outward sign, save a fraternal embrace. Each one will dedicate his or her life to the silent loving of their neighbour, environment and planet, whilst carrying out their daily task, however exalted or humble.

It recognizes the supremacy of the great idea which may only be accomplished if the human race practices the supremacy of love.

It has no rewards to offer, either here or in the hereafter, save that of ineffable joy of being and loving.

It members shall seek only to advance the cause of understanding within whichever church, group or family they happen to be in.

They shall do good by stealth, and teach only by example.

They shall heal their neighbour, their community and our planet.

They shall know no fear, and feel no shame and their witness shall prevail over all odds.

It has no secret Arcanum, no initiation save that of the true understanding of the power of love and that, if we want it to be so, and the world will change but only if we change ourselves first.

All those who belong, belong. That is the Church of Love.

Many churches, groups, sects are impositions by the few on the many, preying on weakness. The Church of Love is the reverse. It liberates, and promotes individual strength. Such vestigial structure as it eventually may have, must come from those who know they are part of it.

Channelled by Colin Bloy, April 1985.
www.fountaininternationalmagazine.com ©

Appendix 4

Mutation of Consciousness, Harmonic Convergence, Crop Circles, Russia and All That.

Quite a long time ago Fountain International came into being based on dowsing observations as to how the so-called "ley-lines" really worked and what that meant. We were mistaken to confuse them with the "ley-lines" that are physical alignment.

They were based on seven parallel lines or multiples thereof and they linked ancient and modern sites. We understood they were the veins and arteries of GAIA, or the collective consciousness.

As I sought to record in "Dowsing for Ley Lines and the Search for the Holy Grail" the seven did become an eight after a certain event at Glastonbury Abbey and the new eight chakra appeared. (Described in the book "Who'd Have Thought It." Colin Bloy and Suzanne Thomas)

At the Harmonic Convergence in August 1988 the eight became a sixteen and the full panoply of the new chakras was made available. The "leylines" which we now call the pathways of consciousness had sixteen parallels. They are relevant both to healing and the new spiritual dimensions of man – what the Templars and the Cathars may have been seeking to achieve, (but too soon) as dowsing text left at the foot of Montsegur in the Pyrenees states. Alice Bailey to Jung and Hassim, via David Walters came aid and comfort for the general Fountain thesis of community healing and that story is well told in Fountain International publications.

What was also stated in those communications was that the more Fountain and similar networks meditated and visualised community and world healing, the more energy was available to the Spirit of the Earth, Gaia, or even the Elohim, for the formation of crop circles and their evolving message.

The year 1991 has just ended after an extraordinary year of manifestation in the fields. Just as important as any perceived message in the forms themselves is the observation amongst Fountain dowsers generally that the circles and forms not only contained the energies traditionally associated with healing but that they linked in to local churches, megalithic sites and the like and were boosting the pathways of consciousness like crazy – the numbers of parallels increasing up to 600, not low multiples of 16.

If that is a correct observation, and if other references in the book to shifts of consciousness are not mere fantasy, then something wholly joyous is happening and may represent a new dimension in mankind's spirituality, opening up a future we may only dimly perceive.

Some readers of Fountain Magazine will know of the happenings at the tomb of Karl Marx in Highgate in 1978. In August 1991, given the coup in Russia, it was seen fit to visit the site again. It was as we left it and one may suppose that the 1991 coup was not ideological but simply a desire not to relinquish power by those who wielded it. I had the pleasure of spending the day after the coup had been defeated with two Russian Naval cadets from a ship in Barcelona. They said that they only unhappy man aboard was the KGB representative. Lots of laughter – open a bottle of Spanish Champagne – hugs all around.

A phone call to Eric Bossard in Michigan U.S.A. He was at the founding of Fountain, a pleasantly eccentric Minnesotan.

"What's going on with the lines? Its all gone crazy."

"Don't you know about crop circles?" I asked.

"Sa-a-ay, is tha-a-a-t what it's all about."

Maybe it is.

If I am right, hold tight for the beginning of the most exciting new dawn for the future of mankind and let us quickly link arms and spirits around the world to create a new archetype of mankind that is spiritual, loving and community orientated. It will fill the void when Western Liberal, Capitalist man who may think that the battle is over, wakes up to the fact it has won nothing. It has just gained a new liberated partner in exploring our future destiny which is neither Marxist or capitalist, but loving, responsible and transcendental and which will be a voluntary return to the collective as free individuals in pure love.

And that, I hope, is the real healing of GAIA, our Mother.

Appendix 5

Holy Water, The Way Good Stuff Works

In August 1991, Maria-Assunta and I were investigating the area known as Barbera, just west of Tarragona in Spanish Catalunya.

We started the investigation because we suspected that there had been a Templar Preceptory there, it was strong Templar country, and indeed we found it at the village of Barbera, the county town, and its surroundings dowsed out just like Shipley in Sussex, where in a sense it all began, described in the "Who'd Have Thought It" book. The final proof was when at lunch time, we ordered a bottle of "Cava", the Spanish Champagne. Apart from being delicious and costing £1.80 per bottle, it was called "Cava de la Commanda." Around the neck was another label, it included the Templar Cross in a medallion and around it read in Latin "The Seal of the Templar Preceptory of Barbera.

As a matter of interest, what first caught our attention on the map was the name Barbera, and nearby another village called Blancafort, (readers of Holy Blood, Holy Grail" will understand why,) and apart from what I shall now relate is a good reason to suppose that more mysteries remain to be discovered.

On the first day of our visit, Maria, who had been born in the village of Garral nearby, took me to the shrine and church of the healing saints – Los Sants Metzges in Catalan – Saint Damien and Saint Cosmo, who came from Syria to Catalunya in the fourth century, performed healing miracles, laying on of hands etc., and were martyred for their trouble. The shrine was built quite recently, is contemporary in style, and made up substantially in a very aesthetic way of old agricultural implements. Why did the Templars come to the land of St Damien and St Cosmo? Perhaps dowsing will give us some more insights when we unravel what is all around the castle of Barbera on its invisible blackboard. Ever ready for more mysteries in this magic land. Maria Assunta remembered that recently there had been rumours in the village of some recent Marian goings-on near Garral, but in the direction of the shrine of the Saints. "Let's go there". I said one Sunday. We were not even sure where it was.

Having stopped where we believed it might be, we were about to go when, following a line I suddenly saw that in a cleft below the road there was a shrine to the Virgin. We went down. It was very new, still under construction; in the cleft was a plastic pipe out of which came a constant flow, not great, of water. There was an "old style" 64-bar line running down the cleft in the landscape. The statue of the Virgin was inside a locked miniature chapel, protected by glass. As we had just been noting the new energy was running by hundreds, we felt it was good to invoke that energy, and it went to 5 X 100. We had first noted these lines in hundreds after the crop circle had really manifested in 1990, and later in 1991, it seemed to be cropping up in various places in different countries – Mont St Michel in France, Barcelona, etc, and when Richard Andrews, dowser emeritus, and I were being fairy lights at the Salisbury Festival of Light, we both agreed that this new energy was on the church near to the Festival venue.

We were not sure what it meant, but it was obviously positive, good and expansive, and it was tempting to see it as another feature in what is perceived to be a great consciousness shift.

When Maria and I spoke later to the organisers of the little shrine near Garral, they indicated that the following day, according to revelations to a local priest, a healing miracle had been promised, and a number of sub-normal children were coming. Hy were they interested? We explained and were immediately invited to the home of one of the, Amadeo, where he showed us a video recently taken in which the foot of the statue Mary in the shrine could be seen to move, like a living foot!!

Someone then asked us for a healing, and another and another, and word got around the village and the room filled up. "You must definitely come tomorrow," they said, and we did. There were around 3,000 people in this little hidden cleft. TV cameras and so on.

The 5 X 100 line started to expand by up to 100 yards across – difficult to count the number of 100s with so many people about.

The friends of the day before came and talked. As the saying of the rosary continued, others came for healing. The priest to whom came the revelations was there, (we later learned he had been "exiled" there for being unorthodox.) When I joined the crowd around him. I felt a hand enter into mine, and I looked down to find a girl kissing it. I gave her my attention and saw that she was one of the ones to whom a miracle had been promised. TV cameras tried to home in, but we would have none of it – it was not right and most embarrassing.

I brought some of the water away, and I immediately noted with my own hands that whenever the bottle was opened, the energy was tremendous. Then thought to observe the effect on someone's field when they drank it. You could feel the first energy body double its size and vitality, and the crown chakra expand, then all the chakras come into harmony, and the effect lasts for several days. It seemed to be homeopathic, as several drops of water in a litre or ordinary water had the same effect as the original water.

The people who took part in the experiment all said they felt good, and the effect at the time of writing is seven days old with a slight reduction to what might be called normal.

On the 29th September 1991, a service to St Michael, to remember the anniversary of the founding of Fountain International took place, and I took a bottle to Rosalind Smith, who was to be there. She is a Radionics practitioner and I wanted her opinion. Luckily John Walker, another, was there.

Three days later I got the following letter. "Both John and myself were regenerated by its properties.

The ray is nine or gold, the gold of divinity.

The Christ coming is increasingly making its presence felt this tremendous inflow has already begun to make its impact on all levels of creation.

We can therefore look for the raising of Lazarus from the "dead" and the emergence of humanity out of the tomb of matter. The hidden Divinity will be revealed. Steadily all forms will be brought under the Christ spirit and the consummation of love will be brought about."

Well that concorded with what I was beginning to think about things generally.

For those who are interested, Rosalind suggests it be used in treating virtually anything, as it is beyond the seven rays of Alice Bailey, and it works on the spirit and higher planes, it may be broadcast at a distance radionically, which raises huge implications. It could be called a remedy that works beyond the soul.

On opening a bottle in my own centre, the existing lines multiplied beyond recognition and the concentric circles in the column of light as well.

Back to Barbera. The cleft of the Virgin is connected to the church of St Michael in the hilltop village of Fores. We found the key with a helpful lady who took us around. She knew Maria's family and was very helpful. There was a statue of Mary above the altar accessed by two sets of stairs on either side. We went up and immediately noticed that it was called, "Our Lady of Healing"! – there was a strong column of light upon it. I noticed that if you went through the curtained area, you could go behind the altar and underneath the statue. The energy was there – the dragon energy of vitality of the first energy body.

Another local had joined us. He had an arthritic condition of the spine, and the spine had no energy. We encouraged him to go in. When he came out, the spiritual energies were as they should be without any intervention from us! We told the lady it was a place of healing. What might that start?

On the way back to Barcelona, Maria said, "I think that the Fores on the mountain is for the healing of the body, and the spring of the cleft is for healing the spirit. That's why they are connected." "I'm sure that you are right." After all, people could go to both for a complete healing, and then they could go to the Sanctuary of St Cosmo to springs with curative properties for a real relaxation – they are in the next village. Would be a wonderful healing pilgrimage.

"Yes," I said. "It could become famous, and it's so new that there is a chance one can learn from other mistakes and get it right. Anyway, the Templars of Barbera would have been pleased.

Appendix 6

Letter From Carmen Marcos

I first came to know Colin Bloy in Toledo at Corpus Christi in 1983 at a healing course he organised.

I am a nurse and I knew little of alternative medicine.

I went to Toledo to learn, my intuition said there was something to learn, and I also hoped it would help me in the arterio-sclerosis from which I suffer.

We met in the lobby immediately on arrival, he was with John Leslie. From the beginning, they both seemed to be profoundly human, mature people, but with something else, they seemed to be full of light.

From then on I realised that people who practise spiritual healing understand cosmic love and radiate light. I became interested in the different sorts of spiritual healing.

I became aware of the serious and meticulous work of the healer, checking thoroughly the physical body of the patient, feeling the illness with their hands, and then healing through them, reinvigorating defective organs with vital energy.

Colin said the energy of the Holy Spirit can come through the hands, passing through us via the crown chakra, making us channels and the instruments of healing.

Two years later, I came to another course with Colin and John.

I saw them work again intensely, and saw the interest of those they were teaching. I saw the great love and the desire to share among them all.

Somehow our lives took on new dimensions, and our love for each other.

Colin always said that healing should be quite natural like any other human act. But to me it still seemed a transcendental act, with great responsibility, and sometimes what I saw made my hair stand on end. But I later understood that it was all a question of letting oneself flow.

Later Colin came to Salamanca for the first time. He gave a lecture in the town theatre. There were many who were interested and asked for healing.

He started to come every month. At the beginning 20 or 30 people came, most of them for reasons of curiosity, wanting to know more, and all with a spark of hope.

It was soon clear to see their improvement after healing. It was different, untouchable but clear. People were amazed and came back full of happiness and faith.

Colin, with his smile and his hands as the only visible instruments was able to give help and hope to the people, for many of them, who sought it.

I remember in those early days, one person with a malignant tumour who, after his operations had been written off as having no hope. Yet from the first time Colin treated him he started to get better and today lives a completely normal life.

Colin always surprised me with the great love he had for everybody, he was affectionate, tireless and completely open, and totally disinterested financially.

From this small group at the beginning, the number of patients slowly increased to over a hundred a day.

It was so great, we had to limit it to 60 -70 a day, with preference to the more serious.

It was an extraordinary phenomenon, for me unique and a privilege for me to take part in it. I often asked myself why Colin came to Salamanca, and why I was the organiser.

There were difficult moments in which I nearly gave up, as I did not have much money, and then more friends joined me and helped and made it possible for me to continue.

As coincidence does not exist and everything has a reason for what went on in Salamanca? After three years, we have treated more than 3,000 people, some with great improvements, arteriosclerosis, arthritis, headaches, hernias, depressions and psoriasis amongst many others. A boy who had a serious accident when a crane fell on him. The first time he came, he could only get out of his wheelchair with crutches, and now is working again normally.

We saw many with incurable diseases, hopeless cases, who came to Colin as their last hope. I can say we did not always get the result that we wanted, but there were many cases of complete cure or great improvements.

Sometimes we had to see them die, which was very sad when so much love had been given.

A few days ago, one of them died from an accident which had nothing to do with what she had been healed from. She had fallen in the bathroom and had terrible bruising. A few moments before her death she said to her daughter. "Perhaps Colin will come and take away the pain."

How can we explain the phenomenon between the healer and patient in the act of healing?

The healer consciously makes himself a channel for energy, giving what he receives. There is no doubt but that it come from "above." You must ask to give. It is Will guided by Love which moves you and makes you the instrument of healing.

Be patient, too, should be conscious of what he needs, and co-operate with love, faith and hope with the healer.

At this moment, a column of light comes down, the energy of the earth comes up and they combine together.

The patient, too, abandons himself to the act of healing and rejects his own ego.

I remember the case of the deaf man who came to Colin. After healing, he could hear again, and threw away his hearing aid. He heard perfectly for two or three months before his deafness returned.

Helping Colin I saw many such people and much love.

All this contributed to creating a new dimension to my life, fuller, more humane.

I have been a witness to many things I did not believe possible in the beginning.

Appendix 7

Recent Comments from Angel Garcia, Barcelona.

Angel Garcia from Barcelona, who has attended several courses and is now a practising healer, has made the following pertinent comments in a communication dated August 1991.

"To be a spiritual healer requires the ability and desire to be a channel to heal our fellow human beings and also our environment, without necessarily renouncing our own individuality.

I am a part time spiritual healer. By that I mean, that whereas I try to be totally professional. I do not earn my living that way. In any event a healer is a healer, which implies that one is a healer 24 hours a day, seven days a week and is ready to heal at any given moment.

For me, this offers no particular difficulty. On the contrary it is a source of considerable satisfaction. I can help someone wherever I am and whenever the person who needs help may be. This is one of the advantages spiritual healers have. Unlike physical surgeons, we can take our work home. We may heal just as easily if the person is with us or many miles away.

This does not require any special preparation or prolonged concentration. A few seconds suffice, and I can start to heal as soon as my working day has finished, or in my mid-day break.

Healing does not tire you, indeed for me and others I know at the end of a healing, the healers feel refreshed and with more energy than when he started.

The energy used in healing is neither strange nor surprising, it is completely natural. I can feel it, just as if I touch a material object. Other healers feel heat, cold or a tingling sensation. In all cases it is an agreeable feeling, a lightening of the body and a clearing of the mind. When I heal it is as if I am watching myself. Although my words and gestures are spontaneous, at the same time, I can see that they adapt to the necessities of the person being healed.

Many types of people come for spiritual healing. Some do not really understand the details before they come, but because a friend told them of it, they come with a certain confidence. They do not have to believe it really works for them, but they have seen it does for the person who has sent them.

They can have very serious problems like cancer, AIDS, chronic infections or bone disease. They can come to be rid of a phobia or to be healed of conditions they do not think they can explain to doctors.

Experience indicates that healing works for all of them. Nor is necessary for people to tell me what is wrong. Working on the energy bodies I can find the cause of the problem and what it is.

I always explain to the person what I propose to do and ask their permission to continue. I feel uncomfortable interfering in the intimate relationship between a sick patient and their illness and need permission to separate them. Once the healing has been carried out, switch off your mind. What is done is done. The effectiveness is not improved by continuing to think about the problem.

In many cases the illness disappears immediately. As with one patient who had a muscular condition and was having regular massage sessions but not getting any permanent relief. After one healing session the pain disappeared instantly and permanently. Such cases are frequent in healing. In other cases, the cure takes a little time. Indeed, it may be a few days before it becomes apparent. Not everyone is identical in absorbing the energy. It is worth noting that, although we may not touch a sick person, they feel the energy pass to them.

The energy does not diminish with distance, nor does the person need to know that I am sending healing. On numerous occasions I have been able to diagnose at a distance from home. It has been successful at 600 miles, making a correct diagnosis of the difficulty and learning later of the great improvement. Without the person knowing that I was working on them at that moment and with the improvement continuing.

In my time as a healer I have treated many people of all ages and conditions. Many were healed, many had great improvement or had their recovery speeded up. In all cases they reported not just a physical improvement but also a great peace and inner harmony.

There are not just changes at the physical level. After healing one may note a raising of consciousness of the individual. It is so frequent and clear that many people request spiritual healing for reasons other than physical, for apparently well people see it as a way of raising their consciousness. The act of balancing the energy bodies, harmonising the chakras and archetypes of the persons consciousness appears to create an improvement in their perceptions and access to new psychological and spiritual dimensions.

These need not imply great changes in daily life, although many feel a great sense of security and a clear sensation of greater union with the cosmic energy. In some cases those treated have felt a new lightness of body and spirit, as if they could fly. The sensation persists during healing. When it is over, it disappears slowly, leaving behind a real inner peace and even an inexpressible happiness. Those with some experience liken a healing to a deep meditation session.

This aspect of healing is a new field where there is clearly much yet to understand. Healing is not a closed technology, but in constant evolution and new understanding. I always learn something new when I heal, everyone is an individual and always shows me some new facet, that is the great miracle of healing. By helping others, we help ourselves.

Appendix 8

THE LIGHT ATTRACTION

Macarena Miletich

Remembering Colin is one of the most endearing things that can happen to you if you have had the opportunity to be close to his teachings and his healing sessions.

"Look, you better start healing right now, please," he always told us as soon as people commented on their desire to grow up in their spirituality and become healers. Or need some understanding about their lives.

One of Colin's tasks was to inspire people to become healers. His intention was for each student and each aspiring healer to integrate the attitude of healing.

His proposal was towards a new attitude of life. He also continuously united people about a topic, an activity or a project, with the intuition that there was a useful contribution and an interesting benefit between both of them.

I have always thought that he possessed a special perception, a kind of smell about the spirit of people. I am sure he knew certain points about each person and made small changes, almost without you noticing. He always found a point of conversation, the offering of a book or technique that would be attractive to the person, as a starting point.

Remembering all those years in perspective I think that Colin opened a door to humanity. It seemed that he had some access to certain new energies, related to the beginning of this new era: the era of Aquarius.

"The revolution will not be physical but silent" he commented many times, as a new way of understanding the Path of Consciousness.

Are we living in these moments in the development of those new proposals? I think so.

Our babies are arriving "super-sized", sometimes they look like small giants. Their hands and feet ... the penetrating gaze ... it seems that they look at us saying: "Hey, maybe you do not know yourself but ... I do know who you really are ..."

There is an exponential difference with babies in the last ten or fifteen years. How they perceive healing, how they identify positive energies and how they allow the restoration of their subtle field to take place quickly. They seem to have X-rays in their eyes and "know" what we are doing through releasing the birth trauma or improving a family condition. The same with food intolerances or vaccines.

Healing has nothing to do with religious norms or rules. Nor with personal success, neither about the power to convince people about certain issues. Healing has to do with the awakening of the person, understanding himself or herself in a holistic vision. We learned a lot about "matter and energy", for example, the two aspects that make up the human being.

The encounter with the concept of the "Archetype" as a design, related to the level "prior to the material world" was crucial, and it must be said that now it is much simpler. I spent many hours in understanding the scope of so many new concepts... The Sacred Geometry that we now have integrated into the day to day and creative expressions appeared as something immense, immeasurable. Colin made it close and easy. Through etheric touch and the continuous experience of "feeling" it was made real and alive, without any doubt about it, which really "changes your life", according to another expression of Colin Bloy.

We learnt that we could take a deep breath and connect with the Light Column. We united the streams of the spiritual world (cosmic levels) with the Earth's energies (telluric levels). Then we felt immersed and connected with the flow of Life. As we trained in this connection, our life changes completely. It is due to the increase in our sensibility "that is exponential". It's like walking on the beach and going into the sea.

This transcendental experience within our consciousnesses, recovering our extra-sensory abilities, was lived in each workshop with a smile and a joke. You never knew what could happen after a pack of jokes, throughout the session. "Listen, to do a good healing you are authorized to do what is necessary, even a joke!"

Only now, after the practice of so many years, we can realize the depth of these sentences, to reach your own attitude as a healer, with full awareness and ... sympathy.

"Light Attraction", all this could have begun, perhaps, in the tomb of Arturo, in Glastonbury, in that ceremony in which the Aquarian Age was initiated. Light Attraction is the best slogan about this New World, I'm sure. It goes to a direct connection.

No religion, no ego, no fear, no darkness. With this slogan like a flag, healing takes you by the hand and you go into its transparency until you are totally surrounded.

We could say that now we take this flag in our hands and we walk through these years learning how the Archetype's shapes extended, as they are needed. We have the certainty of the new that comes to our hands.

Unconditional love and our level of ethics along with our internal searches and the dimensional experiences that come closer to our understanding, increasingly, are somehow "pushing" very slowly and with much love to each of us, fully involved in the Healing and let us go forward in helping this Process that is around us, which involves the whole planet.

Healing is a "way of life":

"Look, the best thing we can do is put Gaia on the top of the list of priorities."

"Humanity has duties, not only rights: can you help the karma of your brothers?"

"Healing will change planetary consciousness".

England, Spain Germany, Australia, United States ... A kind of "intra-network" has been created, a super-connection of consciousness thanks to the Archetypes. Archetypal family throughout the world!

May I mention some references: Colin's books and the journals he promoted: Fountain Magazine in England, in Australia, the Healing Magazine of Vienna, and Homo Amans in Spain. I have had the opportunity to lead this magazine for a while and the experience has been splendid. We can say that in 1996 HOMO

AMANS was the first spiritual magazine in Spain, with these characteristics, linked with freedom to the activity of Spiritual Healing. The current situation is on the other side, since all the information is now available on the Internet, from all perspectives. But in those moments, it was the great impulse, the great help to initiate a more intimate reflection, more personal and in freedom, outside religious or social parameters in some restrictive points. It must be said that Colin was very proud of all these projects: from each magazine he could only say: "It's like a jewel, that's the truth!"

One of the great discoveries that we have been living is that the spirit of the human being is "made" or "built" thanks to five essences, such as: the masculine essence, the feminine essence; the spiritual essence in itself, the called essence of heaven / earth and the energy of the material world, as necessary "polarities" that allow us to find a balance in a totally energetic, measurable aspect, even if it is not physiological.

Many times, it reminds me of Maria Magdalena and her alabaster candles for perfumes. Can you imagine what it would be like? Five spiritual essences are mixed as five floral essences to create a delicate scent of smell! We are made of mathematical proportions, of geometry, of vibrations and of five wonderful essences that build our spirit. This pack is very important and offers us a lot of information about the interconnection of our inner impulses and how we manifest them in the life we are living.

The deep knowledge of the quantum field is functioning through the Light that arrives in the healing. The figures of sacred geometry of the archetypes are the vehicles (like high-end cars) that sponsor with their speed and structure the permanent possibility of regeneration, restoration and amplification of the subtle energy that helps us to evolve. The Archetypes are the essential etheric companions, always available because they respond immediately to all the requests of the healing hands ... Traditionally it is expressed as follows: - "I always connected with the Column of Light of the Holy Spirit and I will become a good channel through each act of healing", to serve my brothers, humanity and my beloved plague Gaia".

His legacy is linked with his real presence in how the Archetypes of Spiritual Healing continue to grow as Spiritual Science, with its premises and its characteristics. Observable. Objective. Connected. Restoring balance and health. Loving path and Service. We could say that as we notice that love rules more and more, we are living a new "intimacy" with the basic geometrical forms and the new ones that are coming to us through the etheric blackboard. We are living it as a gift of Pure Love that comes to us from the stars.

And here it is! Light attraction opens our hearts again and again through the Pure Love that comes to us in each healing connection. And we reach the goal: find our central point, our Self. Our life purposes.

Maybe we can now choose a new joke, for the next season....

MACARENA MILETICH

HEALER- INSTRUCTOR

AND ARCHETYPES RESEARCHER (2019)

Appendix 9

Contractual Arrangements with Holy Spirit

1) The healer recognises that he/she is an instrument of the healing energies of earth and heaven. He/she does not heal.

2) The healer undertakes to heal whomeverso asks for healing, and to treat all alike, whether friend or foe, stranger or family.

3) The healer undertakes to apply total discipline in the act of healing at all times.

4) The healer will never refuse healing on the grounds of inability to pay, if he or she is a professional, or provide any lesser service.

5) The healer recognises that he or she will always be less than perfect, and asks the Holy Spirit to correct all errors, supplement ignorance, and help the healer to transmit energy as well as possible.

6) The healer is a healer of body, mind, and spirit.

7) The healer undertakes to share their knowledge with whomsoever shall ask.

Signature...

Date...